"Mother Salome has long ago proved herself an adept in the art of story-telling...."

—*The Fortnightly Review*, December 1913

About Mother Mary Salome:

Mother Mary Salome was born Agnes Oates in 1860 in Clifton, England. Her father was William Wilfrid Oates, partner to James Burns in the well-known Catholic publishing house Burns & Oates. She entered the Institute of the Blessed Virgin Mary at York as a novice the same year that Mother Mary Loyola became Superior there, and though Mother Salome later spent many years as Superior at the Institute's Convent in Cambridge, and at the Motherhouse in Rome, the two were nevertheless described as "life-long friends." Mother Mary Salome was decorated by the Belgian government for her aid to displaced Belgian children during World War I, having converted classrooms in Cambridge for their use. In addition to writing several books for children, she took on the work of forwarding the Cause for Sainthood of the founder of the Institute, Mary Ward, and wrote an exhaustive biography of her life for this purpose. In 1928 she retired to York due to ill health, and spent the last years of her life with her dear friend Mother Loyola, even writing her necrology for the convent's records before following her in death a mere six months later, on July 24, 1931.

About *Saints and Festivals*:

Mother Mary Salome wrote a volume of meditations called *The Feasts of Mother Church* in 1904, covering many of the most important feasts of the Liturgical Year. In 1913, she followed up with *Saints and Festivals*, adapting portions of her earlier work for a younger audience. In addition to Christmas, Easter and the stories of well-beloved saints, children will also discover the stories of lesser-known heroes of the Church such as St. Chad, St. Serapion, St. John the Dwarf and St. Hilda of Whitby. Even St. John Cantius finds a home in these pages. Peppered throughout with the imaginative illustrations of Gabriel Pippet, this volume makes a wonderful resource for children to take part in the yearly cycle of the Church.

Take the Child and His Mother.

Saints & Festivals

A Cycle of the Year for Young People

by

Mother Mary Salome

Illustrated by

Gabriel Pippet

2018

ST. AUGUSTINE ACADEMY PRESS

HOMER GLEN, ILLINOIS

Nihil Obstat.

FRANCISCUS M. CANONICUS WYNDHAM,

Censor Deputatus.

Imprimatur

EDM. CAN. SURMONT,

Vicarius Generalis.

Westmonasterii,
Die 14 Aprilis, 1913.

This book was originally published in 1913
by R. & T. Washbourne, Ltd.
This edition ©2018 by St. Augustine Academy Press.
All editing by Lisa Bergman.

ISBN: 978-1-936639-99-1

The dates given for the feast days found within correspond to the calendar of feasts in England during the period when this book was originally written. Some of these feast days have since been moved. We encourage the reader to research each life further in order to discover any such changes.

All illustrations in this book are the original illustrations as found in the 1913 Edition.

CONTENTS

PREFACE

This is a book for boys and girls. All boys and girls of correct principles "skip" prefaces as a matter of course. These words are therefore addressed to godfathers and godmothers on the lookout for gift-books. To them I heartily commend this volume.

It is not everyone who possesses the audacity requisite to see the making of a "Scout" in St. Aloysius. Mother Salome has it (p. 132), and exercises it almost as freely in modernizing other holy personages who appear in her stories. The end, in this instance, justifies the means. To interest children, the saintly heroes must be made to talk and act like real boys and girls, men and women; and their adventures must appeal to the rude but indisputable standard of the nursery. In like manner medieval artists reached the apex of Realism by frank and splendid anachronism—turning ancient saints into knights and ladies, and clothing them in the trappings of chivalry. Only thus is it possible to think of them, not as "far-off, vanished things," but as flowers of grace which God causes to bloom in all countries and in all centuries.

In all centuries, undoubtedly. May we say in all countries? Looking through the lengthy list of "Causes" brought before the Sacred Congregation of Rites in recent years, we, who belong to the "imperial races," have reason to hide our diminished heads. Poor, persecuted, "infidel" France, and the "decadent" Latin peoples are busy harvesting their latest crop of Saints. The imperial races seem either to have lost the tradition of heroic sanctity, or to have neither sense to recognize nor care to record its manifestations. Is not this fact worthy of serious reflection?

For without heroic virtue—without Saints— God's work stands still. In the history of the Church the Saints head every movement that can justly be called Catholic. Not to speak of the Apostles, and the Fathers of the Church, and the Early Martyrs, all heathen nations were converted by Saints; all religious Orders were founded by Saints; all schools of learning were brought into being and nursed by Saints; every great religious revival was wrought by Saints. As for social progress, which is almost our fetish nowadays, what broken human thing has not found a resting-place on the bosom of a Saint?—from the physical wrecks which shock and repel the delicacy of the modern world, even while exciting its pity, to the moral wrecks which the modern world proposes to treat only as diseased brutes.

In England, especially, the call for Saints, or for a Saint, is imperative. "Save me, O Lord, for there is now no Saint: truths are decayed from among the children of men" (Ps. 11:1). Acutely sensible of our gross social evils, we exhibit abundance of goodwill. We have a genius for organization. We pass new Acts of Parliament session after session, each guaranteed to herald in the millennium. We have armies of paid and unpaid workers. We are able to command a ceaseless flow of charitable funds. We issue reams of statistics, and hold numberless annual meetings of a congratulatory character. Some progress undoubtedly is made ; but our progress is outstripped by the rapidity with which fresh miseries and discontent pullulate in the sodden soil of the "submerged" population. The cry is raised for more Acts of Parliament, more money, more workers, more training and organization. It is an infatuation. All of us, including Catholics, need to be lifted out of the rut of mere secular efficiency (so largely inefficient), and to be set on the higher plane of religious inspiration. That is, we need the leadership of a Saint.

Mother Salome proved herself long ago an adept in the gentle art of story-telling. It was a happy thought to delve in the buried treasures of the *Acta Sanctorum* for the materials of this book. Saints can evidently be made as interesting as fairies. And if the nurseries are fed up, as they once were, on the exploits of God's chivalry, is it extravagant to hope that England will be again as she has been described, *"olim ferax Sanctorum"* ("once an island of Saints")?

✠ F. W. Bishop of Northampton.

The following Stories are reproduced by kind permission of the Editor of "The Catholic Fireside."

THE NEW YEAR

NEW YEAR'S EVE, and midnight drawing near! Open the window and listen to the bells ringing, solemn and joyous, over town and country. Why are they ringing? Night is the time for sleep and rest. Why do they quiver in their lofty towers and bespeak attention when men are weary? Quick, quick, the Old Year is dying. Let us fall on our knees and let us burden its speeding away with fervent prayer for pardon, acts of loving contrition, loving acts of thanksgiving. We have received much from God—graces, helps, and comfort. We have offended often, falling from frailty, from passion, from sinful habit. Come, let us, weak children, make all right with our Heavenly Father. Let us come close to Him and believe in His mercy and love. For this is why the bells ring out tonight as the Old Year goes by, that with sorrow and gratitude we may wipe away our errors and our sins. "Be merciful, Lord, to me a sinner," is the burden of our song.

Midnight strikes, and still the bells ring on. Why do they not cease with the Old Year? No, they may not cease yet; they have done but half their task. Ring out a joyous peal; the New Year is coming, a gift fresh from the hand of God, like a parchment rolled, unsullied, unmarked by good or bad. The bells promise this New Year to me—my tenth, twentieth, thirtieth, sixtieth—mark the "my" word. But how much will be mine? I am living now, and have seen the Old Year out, but shall I be here at the close of the New? Shall I see the whole parchment unrolled and make my marks upon it as I did last year—good, bad, indifferent, poor, like a careless child's copy? I can get no certain answer to this question. No one on earth can tell me how much of the New Year is to be mine. The doctor may say my heart is sound and my constitution good, but these will not keep me from fever, contagion, or accident. What must I do, then? Bring home to myself this truth of uncertainty, and let it teach me to be wary in my doings and heedful of my steps.

The midnight hour with the merry bells ringing is a time for reflection. I see myself standing and listening to the sound, reaching out my hand to my Creator and taking from Him time in drops, as it were; lifting up my face to Heaven and expecting the hours and the days as they become due. What a hold God has on me! What if I should reach out my hand in vain? What if I lift up my face and receive no light? He is Lord and Master, and the moments are His. Blessed be His Name for ever.

But the bells ring hope into my soul, and joy in the present, and trust in the future. What is best is given always—what is best for *me*. And He Who did not fail me in the past will not fail me in the future. I will take, therefore, from His hand a long life or a short one; joy or sorrow, ease or pain. And I will welcome each as a gift from One Who loves and Who knows. And I will stand up firm and brave to meet the unknown New Year, for I know He will not try me beyond my strength; He will not give me a "stone when I ask for bread" nor a "serpent when I ask for fish."

Now I want all you children to make one resolution at the beginning of this year. But first of all I will tell you a story. Perhaps you know it. Never mind; read it again.

One day, when St. Edmund, Archbishop of Canterbury, was a boy, he was walking alone in a meadow thinking of God and holy things. He loved to go about alone and to think. As he strolled along the fresh green grass, he met a Child of most wonderful beauty. The Child called him by his name, and He spoke as if He was one of his familiar companions. Edmund was astonished. He had never seen the Boy before, or certainly he would not have forgotten such a face. "Do you know Me?" said the Child. "Why, I am with you all day long, always by your side. Look at My forehead, and read what is written there." Edmund read: "Jesus of Nazareth, King of the Jews." "That is My Name," the Divine Boy continued. "And because I love you so dearly, I would have you write upon your forehead every night before you go to sleep these letters—'I.N.R.I.' I will protect you, and keep you from a sudden and unprovided death. And I will protect not only you, but all those who do in like manner." Ever afterwards Edmund signed his forehead with the holy letters, and hundreds of children have followed his example. I would like you to have that practice for your own and never forget it, no matter how tired you may be. It only takes a second or two. Write "I.N.R.I." as you say, "Jesus of Nazareth, King of the Jews, preserve me from a sudden and unprovided death." I know someone who traces the letters three times over for her three brothers, for fear they should forget the act of devotion they used to do together in the nursery. I don't think Our Lord could disown a child who always wrote those words upon his forehead every night before going to sleep.

This is my one resolution. It isn't asking very much, but it will test your faith and your love and your perseverance. Try it; be faithful, and I promise you that it will make a difference in your lives.

THE EPIPHANY

IN a hospital in Germany there were many poor sick people. Some of them could move about, but were not well enough to be discharged. A crib was set up for them, but visitors were allowed to come and pray by the little manger too. The crib took up all one side of a large room, and was very pretty, but rather puzzling, and I will tell you why.

There were three parts to the exhibition. One scene represented the manger with the ox and an ass, with Our Blessed Lady and St. Joseph, and the dear little holy Child. The three Kings were there—Melchior, Caspar, and Balthasar. There was nothing puzzling about them. But in another part of the scene Our Lord was grown up, and was represented standing in a brook of running water; near Him was St. John the Baptist in the act of baptizing, and over the Divine head hovered a spotless dove. In yet another scene was a marriage supper; guests were sitting at table, and waiters were on the watch. The six stone water-pots showed it to be Cana of Galilee, but what had Cana to do with Christmas and the Epiphany? I will tell you what.

Epiphany means *manifestation*, and manifestation means *showing forth*. Now, there were three special times when Our Lord showed Himself forth. The first time at the Epiphany to the Wise Men from the East, whom He brought to His feet by means of the bright star. The second time was at the Baptism, when Jesus stood in the river, and the Holy Ghost, in the figure of a dove, and the Eternal Father by a voice from Heaven proclaimed Him to be His Beloved Son. And the third time was at the marriage feast of Cana, when, to please His most holy Mother, Our Lord Jesus performed His first miracle, even though the real time for miracles had not come.

These are the three Epiphanies, three manifestations that the Church keeps today—January 6. But we usually think of Kings only, don't we, and their grand coming: Melchior with his gold:

> "Born a King on Bethlehem's plain,
> Gold I bring to crown Him again;
> King for ever, ceasing never
> Over us all to reign."

Caspar with his fragrant incense:

> "Frankincense to offer have I,
> Incense owns a deity nigh;
> Prayer and praising, all men raising,
> Worship Him, God most high."

Balthasar with his bitter herb:

> "Myrrh is mine, its bitter perfume
> Breathes a life of gathering gloom—
> Sorrow, sighing, bleeding, dying,
> Sealed in the stone-cold tomb."

Did we bring our offering to Our Lord with the shepherds on Christmas Day? Had we saved up pennies to give to His poor, or to His Church, or to His Vicar on earth? If not, might we not try to bring Him something with the Kings? Ashamed, are we, because their gifts were costly and ours are not? Oh no! We have not gold, perhaps, nor costly gums, nor soothing myrrh. But these gifts were symbols, too, and we can have the gold of charity paid out in word and deed and thought; the incense of prayer, burning sweetly in aspirations and loving words to Our Lord; the myrrh of self-denial, little things suffered joyfully for His sake. Such are rich gifts in our little Master's eyes.

> "Glorious now behold Him arise,
> *King* and *God* and *sacrifice*;
> Alleluia, Alleluia!
> Earth to the heavens replies."

—STAINER'S *Carols.*

"WE THREE KINGS OF ORIENT ARE"

Four Scenes in One Mystery

First Scene: A road winding from east to west over an arid plain, through sunny valleys; a troupe of riding camels, followed by sumpter mules with the baggage; a glistening star in the bright, clear sky; a crowded city and a gaping crowd of people.

Second Scene: A richly adorned room with silken hangings, deep divans, overpowering perfumes; a King standing restless and forbidding; scribes poring over scrolls of discoloured parchment.

Third Scene: The same. The King seated, affable and bland, but with a dangerous look in his eye. Before him, in graceful, attentive attitudes, three high-born strangers, from the Far East apparently.

Fourth Scene: A scantily furnished room in a cottage at Bethlehem; a babe's cot in a corner; homely utensils on a table; in the centre, a child-mother seated on a low stool with a lovely Infant in her arms; behind, leaning over her shoulder, a young man with a strangely pensive face and calm, reserved manner; prostrate, adoring, three gorgeously dressed Eastern strangers, offering gifts.

Scene I.

The Wise Men left "their home, their people's tents, their native plains." They had seen the star, and had set out to track it on its course; they had needed no word of invitation; "a speck in the midnight sky, uncertain, dim, and far," was enough for them, and when its light was dim they boldly asked in the tyrant's city: "Where is He that is born King of the Jews? For we have seen His star in the East, and are come to adore Him."

Scene II.

"And King Herod, hearing this, was troubled." He assembled together all his wise men, and asked them where the Messiah was to be born. They knew perfectly well—not in Idumea, the birthplace of Herod, but in lowly Bethlehem, for they have found the text: "*It is written, And thou Bethlehem of the land of Juda, art not the least among the princes of Juda; for out of thee shall come forth the Captain that shall rule My people Israel.*" Herod dismissed the learned men with little courtesy, and vented his anger upon unoffending slaves.

Scene III.

Herod sat waiting for the three sages. They are coming privately to him. As they enter he bows graciously, and greets them kindly. The star appeared where? how? when? In return for their information, he repeats the intelligence he has gathered from the wise men. The King they seek is born in Bethlehem. Let them go thither, and they will doubtless find Him. But let them not neglect to return and bring the good tidings to him, the King. For he must hasten himself to pay homage to so great a Monarch. The Wise Men listen simply, and leave the royal presence, grateful for the news given to them. But there is no unlocking of treasures, no offering of gifts; Herod is not the King of the star. "Having heard the King, they went their way, and behold the star, which they had seen in the East, went before them, till it came and stood over where the Child was. And seeing the star, they rejoiced with exceeding great joy."

Scene IV.

"And entering into the house, they found the Child with His Mother, and falling down they adored Him."

"And they have knelt in Bethlehem! The everlasting Child
They saw upon His Mother's lap, earth's Monarch meek and
  mild.
His little feet, with Mary's leave, they pressed with loving
  kiss—
Oh, what were thrones! oh, what were crowns to such a joy
  as this!"

Now is the time to open their treasures, to bring forth all that is richest and best, presents typical of the land they come from; typical, too, of the Messiah they have found—gold for the Christ-King, frankincense for the Christ-God, myrrh for the Christ-Man.

"One little sight of Jesus was enough for many years,
One look at Him, their staff and stay in the dismal vale of
tears.
Their people for that sight of Him, they gallantly withstood,
They taught His faith, they preached His Word, and for Him
shed their blood.

"Oh, glory be to God on high for those Arabian Kings,
These miracles of royal faith, with Eastern offerings;
For Caspar and for Melchior and Balthasar from far
Found Mary out and Jesus, by the shining of a star!

"Let us ask these martyrs, then, these monarchs of the East,
Who are sitting now in Heaven at their Saviour's endless
feast,
To get us faith from Jesus, and hereafter faith's bright home,
And day and night to thank Him for the glorious Faith of
Rome."

—FATHER FABER.

HERMITS

St. Paul, January 15

"LET US BE HERMITS, if we cannot be martyrs," St. Teresa said to her little brother Roderick. They had both been trying to find the land of the Moors, so that they might die for the faith. But their uncle found them instead, and brought them back to breakfast.

So, to console themselves for this disappointment, Teresa and Roderick tried to build themselves little huts in the garden. They heaped stone upon stone, and were very much surprised to find that the heaps rolled over and fell about. Then they tried to be hermits without any cells, and this they managed for a little while.

Three Saints who all were hermits keep their feast very close together—St. Paul, who is like the father of all modern hermits, St. Anthony, and St. Macharius. And it is about SS. Paul and Anthony I am going to tell you today.

Paul was an Egyptian of good birth; he had lands and money. When he was fifteen the persecution under Decius was raging, and Paul made up his mind to flee. He was a comely boy, lithe and well built, strong and vigorous. He saw the terrible temptations to sin around him, and he feared his own strength. The persecutors tried the servants of God in two kinds of ways, and I don't know which was the worst to overcome. One was torture and cruelty; the other was the flattery of the senses, inciting to wicked pleasure. Paul may have feared both kinds of temptation; he certainly feared the pleasures. When he was twenty-two he left all his property, and walked straight into the desert of the Thebaid, where the deep yellow sand glitters like dull gold in the burning sun; where only here and there at long intervals a precious spring nourishes palm-trees, and huge rocks shelter beasts from the glaring heat.

It was in a hollow cave that Paul found a cell already made for him. Money-coiners' instruments were lying about, signs of burnt-out fires were scattered around. So the cave had once been inhabited. Where the wicked could live for unholy works, the good might live for holy deeds.

Paul lived in this cave for ninety years! Think of that! He ate dates as long as the tree bore fruit, and then God sent him a raven, who brought him half a loaf every day. Picture to yourself young Paul in his flowing Eastern garment and turban, his sandalled feet, his rich, brown complexion, and dark hair and eyes. Think of him out there in the burning desert, with not a soul to speak to, all absorbed in God, only doing just enough work to keep himself from idleness. The rest of his time he spent in adoring and praising and loving God. What does that sound like to you, who love games, and activity, and pleasure, and fellow-men? Most likely you will never be called to live such lives. But, dear children, remember that the time so spent is not wasted, nor does it pass in misery and gloom. God alone can fill our hearts, human though they are.

Far away in another part of the forest lived a very holy man called Anthony, who was ninety years of age too. One day he had a thought of vanity, and supposed there could be nobody quite so recollected as himself. God sent him to find out his mistake. He led him through desert paths to Paul's cave. This Anthony knew by the shining light that issued from the chinks of the door. He knocked hard and long. At last Paul answered his call. He opened the door and stood on the threshold; when he saw the stranger he stretched out his arms, and a beaming smile lit up his beautiful face. Like brothers long parted, the two Saints greeted each other, and called each other by his Christian name, as if of long acquaintance.

When dinner-time came, Paul and Anthony sat down on the well-worn slab of stone, waiting for his raven messenger. Soon a dark spot was seen on the clear sky, and in a moment the bird flew under the archway and laid a whole loaf of bread at Paul's feet. The good old man's eyes filled with tears of joy. "Our good God has sent us a dinner. In this manner I have received half a loaf every day these sixty years past; now you have come to see me Christ has doubled His provision

Gabriel Pippet 1'39

Hermits.

for His servants." Then they talked of many things, and spent the night in prayer. Next day Paul sent Anthony away on an errand, because he knew he was about to die, and he did not want to distress his friend. Are not Saints unselfish? When we are ill we like to keep people about us; we don't like to be left alone much. It is a thing we have to try and remember, when we are feeling poorly not to bother everyone around us, just as if sickness made us very important, because really it does not.

Well, when Anthony got back to the palm-tree and went into the cave, he found Paul stretched out upon a stone ledge, his hands crossed upon his breast and a heavenly look of peace upon his white face. Anthony now knew what the vision which he had seen on the way meant. He had seen a heavenly company coming to meet a happy soul on its way to Heaven. Anthony prayed long and earnestly by the still dead body, and as he prayed two lions came up with grave majestic tread as if mourning for the departed. They tore up the ground with their paws, and made a hole large enough for the Saint's body. Then they went away as slowly and as quietly. St. Anthony carried Paul in his arms, and laid him in the sandy hole which the lions had made. Paul was a hundred and thirteen when he died. His teeth were perfect, his senses sound, his heart young. It is good keeping company with God, isn't it?

THE WILD ASSES

St. Anthony, January 17

S T. ANTHONY was dead, and Hilarion wanted to go and see the dear old spot in the desert where he had first seen and loved the venerable old Saint. So he set out, and travelled long and far until he came to the desert in Egypt. Then he found his way to the spring and the little river and the big rock where the Saint used to live. There he found two disciples of Anthony. They were named Isaac and Pelusius, and they greeted Hilarion very warmly because they knew he had loved their old master. They showed him every spot sanctified by the Saint, and told him of all he did in each. Here he sang God's praises, they said; here he took his scanty meal; there he cultivated the vine; and that bit of garden he planted and watered with his own hands; this old hoe was his tool, and it had served him for years. Hilarion kissed the holy places, and prayed to the dead Saint to help him to persevere in his hard life.

One little garden was particularly loved by the Saint, his disciples said. It was sheltered by a shoulder of rock, and it was near enough to the water to be easily irrigated.

One day there trooped into this enclosed ground a herd
of wild asses. They scampered all over the place; they
trampled the vegetables, and they ate all they could reach
and did more damage than hundreds of ill-mannered
boys could have done, and I can't say more than that.
Now, you would imagine that it would be of no manner
of use to talk to asses, to say nothing of wild ones. But
St. Anthony thought differently. He went up to the
foremost ass and laid his stick smartly across his back,
and said: "Why do you eat what you do not sow?" The
wild creatures hung their heads, and looked foolish and
ashamed. They slunk away one by one. But they were
not sulky; and to show they did not resent the snub they
came back next day, and ever after; but they never did
any more harm. They drank from the bubbling spring,
and bathed their feet in the rivulet, and spared Anthony's
precious little garden. You see, there was a great deal
of good in those asses. They could take reproof. They
did not sulk. You can do almost anything with an ass,
much more with a child, if it will take a scolding well. It
does not matter how wild it is otherwise. But with an
ass or a child that sulks and won't be corrected—well,
I don't quite know what is to be
done. It would require a lot of
considering to find out. So
we won't sulk; it does not
pay, no matter how you look
at it, and it would not be
worth while if it did.

ONE WHO LOVED JESUS

O N THE Feast of the Espousals, January 23, there was born, in the year 1585, a child whose father was the lord of Newby Hall, Mulwith and Givendale. He was a Catholic, and was called by heretics a "recusant."* He could not go to church because Our Lord had been taken from the tabernacles, and His priests from the altars, and His Word from the hearts of His people. So Marmaduke Ward was fined large sums of money, and he paid them; but kept away from heresy. The little child born to Marmaduke was christened Joan, but was afterwards known by her Confirmation name, Mary. She was a devout baby, and her first word was the Holy Name. One day, when she was only just beginning to walk and was helping herself along by means of chairs, she threatened to fall downstairs. Her mother, who was near, called out in her terror: "Jesus, save my child!" And the baby turned round and said, "Jesus!" It was long before she uttered another word.

---

* This was a term used in England and Wales during the 16th to the 19th century for those who refused to follow the established practices of the Church of England. Most were Roman Catholics.

Again, when Mary was much older, she fell and hurt herself so much that she was stunned. But she remembered afterwards thinking that if she could only say the word "Jesus," she would be well. So with much trouble she said "Jesus," and all her pains left her, and she was quite conscious. To the end of her life there was no sweeter word, no name she loved half so well as this holy Name of Jesus. The letters she wrote she began with "Jesus," and ended with it; she blessed with the holy Name, and she pleaded with it. She died repeating it three times.

When Mary was about ten a dreadful fire burst out at Mulwith. Her father was so busy with his men directing their efforts with the water that he did not miss three of his children. But on inquiry, finding that they were missing, he plunged into the burning house, and found the three, Mary and a brother and sister, saying the Rosary with the greatest devotion. Mary explained that she knew that the house was on fire, but she thought Our Lady would never let them all be burnt, because it was her feast day, and so she had contented herself with saying her Rosary.

Mary loved her father passionately, and he was a man to be loved. We have this description of him: "He was famous in that country for his exceeding comeliness of person, sweetness and beauty of face, and activeness, the knightly exercises in which he excelled, and, above all, for his constancy and courage in the Catholic religion, admirable charity to the poor, so as in extreme dearth never was poor denied at his gate, commonly sixty, eighty, and sometimes a hundred in a day to whom he gave great alms; and yet is also famous for his valour and fidelity to his friends." Now this was a father to admire, and Mary would have done anything rather than offend him. One day when she was very little Mary was in the room where he was writing. She and another little girl were playing together. The companion uttered an oath. Mary was shocked. She knew there was nothing her father disliked more than bad language. So to show her horror she repeated the word in a loud voice. Poor little Mary! Her voice attracted her father's attention; he caught what she was saying, but did not know that it was a mere repetition. Quite against his principle, he strode up to the terrified child, and *corrected* her then and there. "Afterwards he heard me speak," she says dolefully. The emphasis laid on *corrected* renders it impossible to mistake the kind of punishment inflicted, especially as we know the rod was not usually spared in the nurseries of those days.

Perhaps you will be glad to know that Mary Ward, as a child, was not perfect by any means. She had faults like yours. She was fond of notice; liked to be praised; gave way to superstition. But how she did fight these faults! To overcome her daintiness she would take up pail and water, and scour the court out; "she washed the linen, cleaned the plate, scrubbed the rooms, and fed the fowl." And all this in the house of relatives, where her position might have been misunderstood. Mary was a beautiful child. An old biographer says of her: "Her features were exquisite, her look angelic, and her modesty sweet and graceful."

But the life of Mary Ward is too long for these pages. You must read it yourself, and see how she grew up and founded a large Religious Order* that has spread all over the world; how she died very near the old Bar Convent, York, where her Religious Children have worked for more than two centuries to do what she did in her life—bring up children to know, love, and serve God. She was a mother you children would have loved, and, please God, some day you will love her. She was always bright, always joyful. She could not bear to see gloom on people's faces. "Be merry!" she used to say; "in these times" (very bad times for her) "mirth is next to grace." "Three things I love," she used to say: "young people devout, old people patient, sick people joyous." Even when dying, Mary praised and blessed God with joy.

---

* The Institute of the Blessed Virgin Mary (IBVM), now called the Congregation of Jesus.

FEBRUARY

THE FEAST OF THE PURIFICATION

February 2

THIS Feast has many names. It is called the Purification because Our Lady, somewhat more than a month after the birth of Our Blessed Lord, came to the Temple to make the poor woman's offering—a pair of turtle doves or two young pigeons—to satisfy a law by which she was not bound. It is called also the Feast of the Presentation of Our Lord in the Temple, because Our Saviour was offered to God by Mary His Mother and redeemed with the five shekels of sacred silver commanded by Moses. It is also called Candlemas Day, because of Simeon's word, "a *light* to the revelation of the Gentiles." To make this beautiful thought come home to us by means of the senses, the Church puts into our hands a burning candle. We see its flame, feel its warmth, and are gladdened by its brilliancy. This light is the symbol of the little Child

Saviour; He is brightness, comfort, enlightenment. We are to carry Him, as we carry the candle, to our homes, and keep Him with us to illumine our darkness, cheer us in coldness, safeguard us in fear. The shadow of Lent is already upon us; very few days more are given to the childhood of Our Lord. We shall soon have to turn to the "Man of Sorrows." But whilst He is still with us in Baby-beauty, let us take Him to our hearts, try to grow in His love, so that when sorrow creeps into His soul and overwhelms it we may be there to share it and to comfort Him.

There is another source of comfort in this beautiful Gospel story. We see Simeon and Anna in extreme old age delighting in God, and God delighting in them. Simeon, "just and devout," has been kept waiting all his years for "the consolation of Israel." Day by day the promise to see the "salvation of God," the "light of the Gentiles," the "joy of Israel," has brought him to the house of God. And day by day the promise was deferred. Youth passed, early manhood, ripe maturity, old age. Then, led once again by the Spirit into the Temple, his eyes saw the "salvation prepared for all peoples," he held in his arms and pressed to his breast the Child Jesus, and in the joy of his heart he sang a canticle that has become the song of joy of departing day and of departing life: a song to be sung when hopes are fulfilled, trust made good, promises kept—a song of overflowing thankfulness. Simeon was old, and had waited years confiding in God, trusting in His Word.

And that Lord, though He kept him waiting, rewarded him even here below with rapturous joy.

Anna, a prophetess far advanced in years, dedicates her widowhood to God, departs not from the Temple night nor day, "by fastings and prayers serving the Lord." And the day of her reward came as it came to Simeon. Her prophetic eyes, like his, are gladdened by the sight of the Little One of Israel; her seer's soul perceives the majesty of the Jewish Babe, and she "confesses to the Lord and speaks of Him to all who look for the redemption of Israel."

And what lesson are we to learn? This: Simeon and Anna in extreme old age are delighting in God; there is no sense of emptiness in their hearts as in the hearts of worldlings; they have not grown disgusted with the Temple and the God of the Temple; there is no cry of despair in their simple hearts such as there was in that of the world's wise man.

We can learn still more, and with greater comfort still. God is delighting in them. See what kind His servants are—"a doting old man and woman," the business man would say. "Oh, get them put aside," he would add; "we cannot do with such in the service; we want muscular hands, quick brains, the strength of youth, the alertness of manhood. These are too feeble; they must make way; they have had their day." And the old man quits his desk and the old woman drops her needle; they are dismissed, and must manage as best they can.

Not so with our God. We see the withered hands of fourscore and four years still raised in the Temple; we hear her works of "fastings and prayers" called in Holy Scripture "serving." She is sent as a messenger "to all that look for the redemption of Israel"—a messenger at eighty-four!

In Simeon's shaking arms is laid the Creator of the world; his trembling lips are charged to break to Mary the news of her coming sorrow; his feeble voice must sing the model thanksgiving song of all time. And he on the brink of the grave!

Do not we who serve God serve a good Master? Need we fear that in our old age, in the days of our weakness, we shall be cast out, put aside? Do we not see that with Him old age is acceptable, that His sanctuary, His service, His rewards are open to the old as to the young, to the weak as to the strong? Oh! we need be very happy in our service, very full of praise and rejoicing: " Glorify the Lord as much as ever you can, for He will yet far exceed; and His magnificence is wonderful."

"We shall say much and yet shall want words, but the sum of our words is, He is all" (Ecclus. xliii. 29).

ST. VALENTINE'S DAY

February 14

"To-morrow is St. Valentine's Day,
All in the morning betime,
And I a maid at your window
To be your Valentine."
—SHAKESPEARE.

IF YOU make out the grammar of this verse, you will be cleverer than most people are. I don't think it has any grammar, and that is not wonderful, for it was sung by a poor young girl who was out of her mind. Ophelia was distracted with sorrow, and went about singing wild snatches of song. Hamlet, her betrothed, had slain her father and cast her off, and the double trouble had unbalanced her mind.

Though the verse has no grammar to speak of, it has sense. "To be your Valentine" meant to be your lady-love for the coming year. It was a custom, come down from pagan times, amongst the common folk, to look out on St. Valentine's Day for a "true love," and the maid first seen in the morning was the one to be chosen. Now this arrangement was often enough very awkward, always very silly, and sometimes even an occasion of temptation. So, gradually, as people gained more sense, and occupied themselves with higher things, they dropped these remnants of heathenism, and contented themselves with sending pictures to each other. Even these pictures, or "valentines," are seldom bought now, and a very good thing too, because they were often vulgar.

But there was a real "Valentine" once, and *he* was a Saint. As you may suppose, he had nothing whatever to do with a pagan custom. He was a holy priest who lived in Rome in times of persecution. His greatest joy was to attend the martyrs in their last moments, and help them in prison. One day he was taken prisoner himself and brought before the judge. Every argument was used to make him renounce his Faith, but he remained firm. Then the sentence was pronounced: Valentine the Christian priest was to be beaten with clubs, and then beheaded. The holy priest bore the cruel martyrdom with perfect patience, and received his crown and palm on February 14.

So there is this connection between the martyr and the pagan custom. He died on February 14, and that was the eve of the day the heathen Romans held their festival in honour of *Februata Juno*, and the time when boys drew the names of a companion for the year. St. Francis of Sales saw the harm the lingering of the old custom caused, so he devised a Christian drawing of names. Children should choose by lot patron Saints, he said, and honour them with special love and devotion all the year round. And this good custom is now observed, not only in France, where St. Francis of Sales lived, but in many other countries also. Couldn't some of you elder ones write the names of your favourite Saints on little slips of paper, as many slips as there are persons in the family, and let the slips be drawn on the eve of St. Valentine's Day? I think you could, and I think that thus you would help to honour the Saints, and they would certainly not forget you in return. The slips of paper might be like this, printed or simply written:

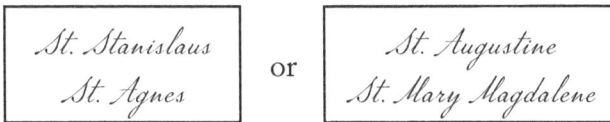

St. Stanislaus St. Agnes	or	St. Augustine St. Mary Magdalene

Or any other names you like. Do you understand?

ST. CHAD

March 2

EVER heard of him before? There were four
brothers, all holy, two of them canonized Saints.
Their names were Celin, Cymbel, Cedd, and Chad.
They lived in the middle of the seventh century, when
St. Aidan was Bishop of Lindisfarne, and St. Wilfrid
apostle of the north. They were peasant boys, but they
were as well educated as if they had been princes. Chad
was sent to Lindisfarne to school, and was taught to
love learning. He loved it so much that he thought
he would travel and learn more and more. And where
do you think he went to become learned? To Rome,
Florence, Paris? No—to Ireland. For this was the
time, or one of the times, when Ireland was like a great
school of knowledge, with masters enough for herself

and to spare. There went from that green isle scholars to every land. So Chad was wise to cross the sea and go west. When he returned, he helped his brother St. Cedd to found a monastery at Lastingham, in the Wolds of Yorkshire. Cedd died of a terrible pestilence that was raging in the north, and left the monastery to his brother. It was a monk's duty to go among the people and preach in the villages, in the towns and hamlets, and at cottage doors, for the peasants were very ignorant; many were pagans, and many were bad Christians. Chad roamed about on foot and instructed the people all day long.

By a mistake Chad was consecrated Bishop of Northumbria. He did not want to be a great man; he loved quiet and humble living. But he was too simple to make a fuss, and submitted quietly when the Bishop consecrated him. When, however, the mistake was found out, and a holy Bishop, St. Wilfrid, had to tell Chad that he must resign his See and leave York, St. Chad only smiled. He was quite content to leave all his honour and to live like a humble monk. So he went back to his monastery at Lastingham, and would have died there humble and happy had not his virtue been found out, and he was made Bishop of Lichfield. He was getting old at this time, and Theodore, his superior, forbade him to go about on foot as he always had done up to now. So Theodore set him on horseback, and told him to spare himself as much as he could.

Chad was always praising God. When the wind blew strong and loud, he praised God. When there was a storm he would go to the church and pray with great fervour. Sometimes people would ask him why he prayed in the lightning and thunder. Then he would tell them of God's judgments, and how sad it would be to die out of His friendship. Whenever he had leisure and his work as a Bishop was done, Chad would go to a monastery he had founded in Lincolnshire, and spend a quiet time with seven or eight monks, his best friends. One day there came to this little house news that a great noble from the Court was going to enter, and that he would be with them in a few days. After the days were gone by, there came to the door a man dressed in a coarse tunic such as peasants wore. In his hand he had an axe and a hatchet. The porter asked who he was. He answered, "Orwini." This was the name of the noble whom they were expecting. Orwini wanted to show that he came to work like a lowly man, not like a noble. He became a holy monk, and ploughed the fields, and did disagreeable things.

One day Orwini, who loved St. Chad like a brother, was cutting wood near the church. He heard the most heavenly singing. He listened; it seemed to be coming down from Heaven. Then it spread, as it were, all over the church; then it died away, and seemed to go back to Heaven. Then he heard Chad's voice calling. "Make haste," it said; "bring the seven brethren hither that they may come and praise God with me. Soon a Visitor will come and take me away." Orwini did as he was told; then he threw himself on his knees before Chad, and begged him to tell him what was the wonderful singing in the church. Chad was astonished that he too had heard it. He said that they were angel voices that he had heard, and that Angels were come to announce his death in seven days' time. Orwini had to promise the Saint that he would not tell anyone this great secret until after Chad's death.

Seven days went by. Then the end came, and the weary old Saint was found waiting and longing for it. The singing was heard again, and some saw in a vision the Saints from Heaven coming down to meet the Saint upon earth, and in the bright company was Cedd, Chad's dear brother who had gone Home so long before him. It was the year 672, March 2, the day the Church now keeps his feast. Wouldn't we like to have a death like that?

ST. THOMAS AQUINAS

March 7

Two babies lay side by side one hot summer's night; they were boy and girl, sister and brother. A terrible storm arose, the lightning flashed and lit up the room, the thunder rolled round the old castle and seemed to shake it to its foundation. Oh! that was an awful flash! And then came a crash as of the last day! Theodora, Lady of Rocca Sicca, opened the door of the nursery quickly. She wanted to see if everything was well with her babes. Thomas was fast asleep, but his little sister was dead. Side by side they had been parted. One was taken; the other left. The poor mother raised the sleeping child, and renewed the vow of its consecration. He was to be a priest; she had consecrated him to God.

Thomas grew up fine and strong and handsome, a child to be proud of, and the Count and Countess were proud of him. When he was five he was sent to the Benedictine Monastery of Monte Cassino. When he was ten the good monks told his father that he knew all they could teach him; he should be sent to the University of Naples. Landulf, the Count, was glad his son was clever, and he took him to the celebrated schools. The men there were wicked, and they laid snares for the child. But Thomas prayed, and avoided all the companions whom he at all suspected of bad ways. His great joy was study—study and prayer together; they seemed the same thing to the boy. One day his master found him sitting in the shade with his head leaning on his hand. He asked him, with surprise, why he was not out playing with the other boys. Thomas looked up and, scarcely knowing what the question had been, answered: "Tell me, master, what is God?" You see where his thoughts were.

Are you thinking that this is the story of a milk-sop? Don't think that. He had more brains than any other man of his time or since; he was brave when there was a question of right and wrong. His brothers wanted one day to take his religious habit away, and they laid violent hands upon him; but he defended himself so courageously that, two against one though they were, they had to give in. Another time a wretched creature tempted him to evil; he caught up a burning torch and drove the tempter out of his presence. His father and mother had destined him to be Abbot of the great Monte Cassino Abbey. Thomas knew that God had called him to be a poor monk, devoted to study. Now, everyone is obliged to obey God first, and his parents afterwards. The boy could not, therefore, obey his father when he wished something opposed to the will of God, so he stood firm to his true vocation. For this Thomas was hunted down, imprisoned, fed on bread and water; he was taunted and insulted by his brothers; his mother, even, had no pity upon him. She was a proud woman, and could not bear to think that a son of hers, the gem of the family, should wear the habit of a Dominican Friar. Thomas was young; he loved the fresh air, the company of his family; he felt hunger and thirst as you do, naturally; he disliked cruel insults; yet he bore all this with silence and perfect cheerfulness. Do you think that looks like a milk-sop or a muff? Anyway, it is not my idea of a muff. A muff is one that will do the will of another, right or wrong, for fear of him; one who cannot bear cold, or heat, or trouble without complaint; one who seeks his own comfort everywhere and in everything—that is a muff, and a real one. But such a one Thomas of Aquin was not.

One day messengers were sent from the Holy Father to the Count of Rocca Sicca. The order was that he should put no further obstacles to his son's vocation; the boy was to be set free and allowed to follow God in the way he had chosen. But now came an adventure. Countess Theodora was a self-willed woman; she did not like yielding, or at least appearing to yield, so she concocted a plan by which Thomas should make his escape. The Dominicans were to come to the castle at a certain day and stand beneath the window of his cell. Most joyfully they obeyed. At the appointed hour they stood where they were directed, and waited and watched. Suddenly a basket was seen floating in the air above them; it dangled against the wall, suspended by a stout cord. Gradually as it was lowered they recognized their young disciple, Thomas, the prisoner. The boy's face was lit up with joy, though he seemed in momentary peril of his life. And when he greeted his white-robed brethren and understood that he was free to accompany them back to the monastery, he was beside himself with delight.

When Aquinas was eighteen he was sent to study at Cologne, where the most learned man of his day was teaching: this was Albert the Great. Everyone in the city had heard of young Thomas as a prodigy of learning, and on his arrival they were ready to do him homage; but Thomas was afraid of vanity, and he determined to hide his great talents. Praise is dangerous; even if it does not puff us up, it sometimes fills our heads with perilous ambition. Besides, Thomas was so full of the love of God that he could not bear to think of dividing his heart. When, therefore, difficult questions were asked, Thomas always appeared as if he knew nothing; when he said his lessons, he hesitated and stammered. The students were much surprised; they had heard his abilities much praised, by people, too, who ought to know. And there he was sitting on the bench dumb or nearly dumb. Some of the smart ones began to call him names and ridicule him. He was the "great, dumb, Sicilian ox," they said, and by that name he became known in the University.

One day, however, Thomas forgot himself. A good-natured student thought Thomas could not master a lesson; he came to him and began explaining. But the explanation was so poor that Thomas helped the explainer, and did this in such a brilliant manner that the good-natured man was amazed. The story went the round of the schools, and people began to suspect the reason of the young student's silence. Blessed Albert put a very difficult question to his class, and ordered Thomas to answer it. The result was wonder and admiration on all sides. "Ah!" Albert exclaimed, "this dumb ox of ours will one day bellow so that the whole world will hear."

Did you ever hear of the friendship of Jonathan and David—how they loved each other as though they had but one soul? Just such a friendship was there between St. Bonaventure and St. Thomas of Aquin. One was a Franciscan, the other a Dominican; but both were Saints and loved each other in God. They used to visit each other in their cells and come in without any ceremony. One day Thomas found his friend writing the life of his founder, St. Francis of Assisi. "Come away," said Aquinas; "let us leave a Saint to write of a Saint." Another time Aquinas asked his friend where he found all his learning. "There," said Bonaventure, pointing to the crucifix. It was an answer that would have done for St. Thomas too.

St. Thomas's greatest love, though, was the Blessed Sacrament. He has written upon this mystery as no other Saint has done. When Urban IV asked him how he should reward him for all the services he had rendered the Church, Thomas answered: "By making the Feast of the Blessed Sacrament a universal feast." It was then only kept in certain places. Urban IV granted his request, and St. Thomas himself wrote the beautiful Office. We sing his verses every day at Benediction— the "*O Salutaris*" and the "*Tantum Ergo*," which are verses taken from his two long hymns, "*Verbum Supernum*" and "*Pange Lingua.*"

Do you notice that great people never show off? It is only the small minds that do. Persons in lesser offices are generally the most consequential. I saw a butcher boy once; he was about twelve and had just been apprenticed to the trade. He had his new apron on and knife-sharpener by his side, and he strutted around amongst the meat as if he was proprietor of the shop at least. Only the proprietor did not strut. Thomas of Aquin was the most learned man of his time, yet he was so humble that he was at anyone's beck and call.

There was a lay brother once who wanted a companion to go into the town with him. He did not know Aquinas by sight, and he called him to come and help him carry the begging-bag. The Saint came at once and shouldered the bag and went out with the brother. All the way the brother scolded. Aquinas limped because he had a bad foot, and the lay brother, being in a hurry, was vexed at the Saint's slowness. When the two got back they were met in the passage by a Father who knew the Saint. He was horrified that so learned a man should have been taken off his writing to go on an errand that a simpleton could have done. But St. Thomas was overjoyed, and only apologized to the poor, discomfited lay brother for being such a long time on the road.

I must not forget to tell you that St. Thomas was a great friend of St. Louis IX of France. The two frequently dined together, and St. Thomas was often so full of deep thoughts that he forgot his Sovereign and everything else—his dinner and his manners even. One day he neither ate nor drank, nor did he speak. A courtier wanted to set him right, but the King would not have him interrupted. At last St. Thomas struck a mighty blow upon the table and exclaimed: " I have it!" It was an answer to one of the heresies of the day. Louis, far from being annoyed, had pen and paper brought that the theologian might put down his thoughts at once.

St. Thomas did not die in one of the monasteries of his own Order; he was on his way to the Council of Lyons, summoned thither by order of the Pope. The Saint was ill when he started, and he died on the way. In his agony he dictated an explanation of the "Canticle of Canticles." When the Holy Viaticum was brought to him, he cried out lovingly to Our Lord: "Thou art the King of glory, Thou art the everlasting Son of the Father!" His very last words of all were those of his own beautiful hymn, "*Adoro Te Devote*."

Is not that a beautiful life, and a beautiful death? There is suffering in it, and trials, and troubles, but there is so much happiness, such joy. Wouldn't we like to order our lives like that? And why not? Of course, we are not geniuses—that does not matter; we can live beautiful lives without talents of any kind. To begin with, let us ask St. Thomas to get us a great love of the Blessed Sacrament of the Altar; and to obtain this favour let us say, with as much fervour as ever we can, those hymns of St. Thomas, the "*O Salutaris*," and the "*Tantum Ergo.*"

ST. JOSEPH

March 19

"Go to Joseph and do all that he shall say to you," said Pharaoh, King of Egypt, to the famine-stricken people who came to buy corn in the land of plenty. This Joseph was the Hebrew to whom God had spoken in dreams, who had been sold a slave into Egypt by his own brethren, but who, because he was "full of the Spirit of God," was made Governor of the land. "Thou shalt be over my house; without thy commandment no man shall move hand or foot in the whole land of Egypt," said Pharaoh the King. "And he clothed him with a robe of silk, put a gold chain about his neck, and a ring upon his finger, and had him proclaimed the 'saviour of the world.' And the Lord blessed the land of Egypt for Joseph's sake." When the years of plenty had passed over the land, the famine came, as predicted, and continued for seven weary years.

Then the very men who sold their young brother into bondage journeyed from Canaan to Egypt. They were starving. Money they had in plenty, but of food they had none, so they stood before the Governor who held the keys of all the granaries of Egypt. And he knew them; but there was no resentment in his heart. "Come nearer to me," he said. "God sent me before you that you might be preserved; God hath made me lord of the whole land of Egypt," and he pressed them to come down with their families and their flocks. "Come down to me; linger not, then I will feed you." And Pharaoh the King added his persuasion: "I will give you all the good things of the land of Egypt for Joseph's sake." Then Jacob and his children and their kinsfolk, their flocks and herds, came down to the land of Gessen, a land apart from the busy cities, and settled there, saying: "Only let my lord look favourably down upon us and we will gladly serve the King."

But there was always a fear in the hearts of the ten brothers. Their crime had been so heinous; they could not believe Joseph had forgiven them. When, therefore, Jacob their old father died, they trembled lest Joseph, having nothing to restrain him, should revenge himself upon them. Such a thought was far from one in whom dwelt the "Spirit of God." "Fear not," he said; "I will feed you and your children." And he comforted them and spoke gently and "mild" to them. He kept his promise with princely munificence.

Such was the man whom Israel loved "above all his sons." We know of another Joseph, a Hebrew likewise, one "full of the Spirit of God, a just man." To the first Joseph it was Pharaoh who spoke, and the dominion given was over a pagan, earthly kingdom. To the second it was God Himself Who spoke, and the dominion was over the treasures of Heaven—Mary, Immaculate Mother, and Jesus, Son of God. The powers of the Patriarch of old were wonderful. God gave into his hands the sustenance of thousands of people. From his childhood upwards He spoke to him in dreams, and was with him throughout his whole career.

To Joseph, son of David, God spoke in dreams likewise; He was with him "all the days of his life." He put under his protection the Virgin Mother and the little Saviour of mankind. It was Joseph who was their protector at Bethlehem, who planned their flight into Egypt, and nourished them there; who chose the place of their home. It was he to whom Jesus "was subject" during the hidden life. If Pharaoh's wisdom was shown in his choice of a governor for Egypt, is not God's wisdom shown in His choice of a guardian for Mary, a foster-father for Our Lord? Will it be hard to guess at the virtues of Joseph, son of David, when we know those of the son of Jacob? The Patriarch was powerful, prudent, mild and gentle, forgiving and long-suffering, true to his word, faithful to his promises. We cannot suppose that the Patriarch of the Gospel, with his high calling, could be less powerful, prudent, or wise, less faithful to his promises, and less gracious. So we will come to him with our little troubles, our hopes and disappointments and our needs, spiritual and temporal, and we will ask him for protection, spiritual food, counsel, and help. He will help us with fatherly love if we trust him with childlike confidence.

"Go to Joseph," is still the command, and "do all that he shall tell thee"—that is, do as he did, be prudent as he, obedient, self-sacrificing, silent and humble as he; then will come to pass that other word: "I will give you all good things for Joseph's sake."

ST. SERAPION

March 21

THERE was a very holy young man whose name was Serapion. His nickname was Sindonite, because he wore only one garment, a coarse linen one. He lived in Egypt, but travelled into many countries to learn how to serve God better. The passion of his life was *giving*. You have heard of people whose passion in life is saving, haven't you? Well, you know what that means. A man who saves and never spends except what he can't help is called a "miser," and very disagreeable misers are, both to themselves and to everyone else—except their heirs.

Serapion's passion was giving, as I said before. I call it a passion, because he gave everything and always; not *things* only, but more—a hundred times more than that. If I did not tell you, I do not think you would ever guess what he gave. He gave himself—that is, he *sold* himself and gave the money to the poor. Greater love than this no man can have for another; for when Serapion was sold, he was a *slave*, one who works for, and belongs to, another, life and limb, having and getting. The man to whom Serapion sold himself first was a comedian, and an idolater; so the Saint had enough to do. He set himself to convert the comedian, and he managed so well that the whole family became Christians. When they were baptized they gave Serapion his liberty, for they looked upon him as their greatest benefactor.

So the slave was set free again. One day he met a widow woman. She was in great trouble; her little children were starving; she had no work; there was no means of getting any food. Serapion's heart was touched with sorrow. He went to the slave market and sold himself as a slave again. The twenty pieces of money, his price, he gave to the poor woman to get herself and her little ones bread. This time he found a good master, a man who was kind to all about him, kind even to slaves. He loved Serapion and admired him; he watched him at prayer and at meals, and liked to hear him talk of his God. Bit by bit his mind was enlightened, and at last he, too, became a Christian. Serapion was again set at liberty, and this time with presents—an under-garment, a cloak, and, what was most precious, a book of the Gospels. In those days books were worth more than their weight in gold, because they were written by hand.

The Saint was now quite rich: he was well clad, he had a precious volume, and the means of gaining a livelihood. But before long he met a beggar, who was badly dressed. Serapion took off his cloak and handed it to the poor man. A little further on he came across an unfortunate creature only half covered. The Saint

gave him his new under-garment and went his way
happily. One of his friends met him, and asked what
had become of his clothes. Serapion pointed to the
book he still held, and told him he heard a voice coming
from it saying: "If thou wilt be perfect, go, sell all that
thou hast, and give to the poor." As he continued his
journey he said to himself: "*Sell all that thou hast!*"—all.
Then even the precious book he held so dear. "*All.*"
Serapion took the book and sold it for the poor. Now
he was Serapion the Sindonite once more, for he had
only the linen garment.

I could not tell you all the times the Saint sold
himself for a slave; it would sound like the story of the
locust and the grains of rice, which I am sure you all
know. But he went in and out of the slave market till
he was too old to be of much use; then he went into the
desert of Egypt and lived all alone, and gave himself up
to prayer for the rest of his days, which were till he was
sixty years of age. At that age God took him to Heaven
to reward him for all he had done for His poor.

Can you think what Our Lord's smile of welcome
would be for a man like Serapion? You know what
Our Lord promises those who give things to His
little ones. To a man like this Saint what would He
not give? and how lovingly He would give it. God is
never outdone in generosity. If we give, He gives. I
know someone who has a purse set aside for the poor,
and she gives and never refuses. Well, that purse is
never empty; it is very nearly empty sometimes, but

never quite. If she didn't give it would often be empty. This is not human logic, but it is supernatural, and quite commonplace at that.

A HERO

St. Turibius of Mogrovejo, March 23

I LIKE to tell you of great men and women, because, you know, "Lives of great men all remind us we may make our lives sublime." And that is what we want to do—at least, I hope we do. My hero to-day is a Saint whose feast is kept on March 23, a Spaniard of noble family, who became an Archbishop and a missioner out in the Far West. His name is long and quite unknown to you, I expect—Turibius—and his father was Lord of Mogrobejo, an estate in the kingdom of Leon, Spain. Alphonsus was the boy's name, and when quite young he showed how much he loved the poor. He would give all he had to relieve anyone in trouble, and anybody might have his dinner. Once a pedlar woman was angry and flew into a passion because she had lost something out of her pack. Alphonsus was upset to see her offend God so easily. He went to his mother, and begged from her money enough to replace what the poor woman had lost. The boy was splendidly educated, and made great progress in his studies. He went to the Universities of Valladolid and Salamanca, and when he

was grown up was made Judge of Granada by Philip II
of Spain, who loved him much.

But Turibius was not meant to try civil offences all
his life. The Archbishop of Lima died, and there was
no one to fill the post. The mission was far off, the
diocese poor, and scattered over an enormous area. It
was in a fearful state of misery and wickedness, and
the climate was trying. Philip II looked round upon
all his prelates and great men, and only one seemed
to him fit for the task. And this one was a layman; he
was not in orders of any kind. But he was holy, and
loved prayer; he was mortified, and sought the glory of
God alone and the good of souls. The King made up
his mind, and Alphonsus was consecrated Archbishop.
You may imagine what sort of preparation such a man
would make for such an office. He prayed and fasted
and did penance. He reached Lima, in Peru, when he
was forty-three years of age, and had to begin all his life
anew, amidst unknown people with unknown tongues,
and in an unknown land. He required a big, brave heart
to set to work in such a new field; but the Saints have
brave hearts, and Alphonsus was a Saint.

His diocese stretched along the coast for one
hundred and thirty leagues; it was scattered over the
Andes, the ruggedest mountains in the world. The
people inhabited huts perched high up on the rocks,
or on the borders of impenetrable forests, or beside
wide-spreading marshes. Any day you might have
seen the Archbishop on hands and knees crawling over

some rocky promontory to reach some old peasant in a cottage, or he would swim a river to get to a lonely hut. Nothing frightened the Archbishop; he confronted wild animals and wilder tribes; he fought for the poor degraded natives against their worst enemy, the wicked white man; he shielded them because they could not shield themselves. For their sakes he brought down upon himself the hatred of the Spanish settlers, who for the most part only thought of gain, and did not care anything about the souls of the native tribes. They used to sell wine to these poor creatures, who would intoxicate themselves with it, and barter in exchange their gold and jewels and precious stuffs—anything to get the fiery liquid. By much patience and love and hope the holy Archbishop made a wonderful change in his diocese. He built churches and monasteries and hospitals. He visited every spot of his little kingdom, and watched over all like a true father. He was seven years making one visitation! But then he left no place untrodden, no poor creature unconsoled.

Perhaps you think that such a man was praised wherever he went, that all his people saw and understood what a lot of good he did, and how unselfish he was and how hard he worked; but this was not the case at all. Of course, there were some who knew what a great man their Archbishop was; but a great many believed cruel calumnies that were spoken about him. Turibius had to tell great men of their faults; he had to show them that he could not allow scandals to go on; he had to be severe when severity was necessary. And the wicked could not bear that, so they turned round upon him, and said what was not true and what was bad of him; but the Archbishop bore all sweetly, and forgave freely.

When Turibius was quite old he learned several languages. You see, some of his people spoke strange tongues, and he could not make them understand his Spanish, so with great courage he set to work to learn languages. That, I think, was grander than going about among rocks and swamps and wild beasts, because, when travelling, you would get the sweet breath of Heaven upon your face, and you would have some excitement in outwitting wild beasts; but to sit down and learn hard new languages, when your memory is not at its best, is, to my mind, real heroism. And that is what our Saint did.

Turibius died like a Saint and a hero. He went to the church to receive the Holy Viaticum. On his death-bed he said over and over again how much he wanted to be with Our Lord. And when he knew for certain that he was dying he cried out: "I rejoiced in the things that were said to me; we shall go into the house of the Lord!" His last words were: "Into Thy hands, O Lord, I commend my spirit!" And then he died.

Wouldn't you like to be a great man like that? So strong and unselfish, doing big deeds for the good of souls and the glory of God.

APRIL

THE WOLF AND THE LAMB

St. Leo, April 11

I AM not going to tell you exactly of the wolf and the lamb; the name is an allegory of a true history, as you will see.

It was the year 423; the Emperor Honorius had left Rome, and had set up his capital at Ravenna, in the north of Italy. Those were bad times. Roman vigour had gone; there was disunion and weakness in the empire. All round—to the north and south, to the east and west—young nations were gathering strength, and banding themselves together to sweep upon the fertile plains of the southern countries. The Vandals and Visigoths were laying Spain waste; Alaric with his band had crossed over and ravaged Italy. He had sailed away down the blue Mediterranean, a conqueror with spoils.

But there was worse to come. In the northeast
of Europe dwelt a tribe of savages, short of stature,
stout of limb, debased in mind. They were called
Huns. They lived in the saddle; ate their meat raw;
neither planted nor sowed, nor built nor wove. Their
ambition was to spread over the face of the earth, to
conquer and devastate, to kill or make captive, as their
fancy took them. Attila was their leader at this time,
and he was a typical specimen of his race. He had a
broad chest, an enormous head, small flashing eyes,
a perfectly flat nose, little hair, and no beard. Such a
commander attracted the admiration of such a people;
he had their characteristic of beauty, and they followed
him proudly.

St. Leo was Pope. He had not fled from the
doomed city of Rome. When the report reached him
that 700,000 Huns were marching southward he held
a council.

And the question he asked was: "What means
could be taken to preserve the city?" An embassy to
the Hunnish leader was the only possible hope left.
But who would undertake it? Who would dare to ask
for terms from that pitiless barbarian, who was bound
by no law? Without a moment's hesitation Pope Leo
stood forth. He would go and sue for grace, he said.

Attila heard of the audacious messenger, and
prepared to receive him with mocking pomp. Leo was
an old man; his hair was white, and his eye had lost
the brightness of youth. But, as the Vicar of Christ, he

spoke with such calm dignity, with such cool courage, that Attila was astonished.

"I cannot imagine why that priest's words have touched me so much," he said. So touched was he, in truth, that he marshalled his barbarians, and carried them off out of Italy, leaving the Eternal City in peace.

Just think what that triumph meant! On one side there were 700,000 unconquered savages, lying before a rich city, in the midst of fertile lands, inhabited by a fascinating race; on the other there stood a meek priest, weak with age, clad in priestly garments, without defence. Yet the old man conquers, because God was on his side, and no mortal foe can resist God.

> "He always wins who sides with God,
> To him no chance is lost."
> —Father Faber.

Think of thousands of barbarians thirsting for blood, waiting only for a sign from their leader to set forth and plunder and kill. Then an old man speaks, and the horde is withdrawn.

"Who art thou?" Leo had asked the Hun.

"I am the scourge of God," he had answered.

"If thou art the scourge of God, thou art welcome, for all that comes from Him is good," the holy Pope had said. But the Scourge of God was turned away for that once by the might of a Saint's prayer. After three years again the Saint appealed to another barbarian, and once again he gained a reprieve. But the day of wrath was only postponed. The time came when the hordes were allowed full scope to vent their fury.

Think of St. Leo on April 11, because the Church keeps his feast that day. If we ask him, he will get us a splendid courage like his own.

SAPOR, THE DIVINE

St. Simeon, Bishop of Ctesiphon, and His Companions, April 17

SAPOR II was King of Persia when Constantine was Emperor of the West. Sapor had been King from his cradle, and to say he was proud would be to express things very mildly. He once wrote a letter to the Christian Emperor, and it began like this: "Sapor II, King of Kings, partner with the stars, brother of the Sun and Moon." The sun and moon were gods, so, of course, Sapor meant that he was a god too, and this he impressed upon his subjects. They were invited to come and worship him, and if they would not he persecuted them to the death. There were at least three separate persecutions in this King's time. You see, he had a very long reign, because he began so early. During the last forty years he killed quite 16,000 Christians.

The Bishop of Ctesiphon was a venerable man called Simeon. He was beautiful to look at, fine, and tall, and strong. This holy Bishop was helping his subjects to defy the wicked King of the Persians, and to hold out against his threats and his blandishments.

Sapor heard of him, and had him sent for to his palace. "Let Simeon, the leader of the wicked men who despise my divinity, be brought before me." Simeon came into the royal presence, and Sapor was much taken with his gracious beauty. He spoke in admiration of him to the courtiers standing about. After threatening the Saint, Sapor dismissed him, hoping to bring him to his senses later on. As the Bishop passed out of the gate of the palace he noticed a man sitting at the entrance. He was the keeper of the King's chamber, and was much loved by the King. For his sake the keeper had once denied his God and worshipped the sun. As Simeon passed by, the renegade stood up and bowed low. Though he was a coward, he honoured courage. But Simeon turned aside, and would not acknowledge the bow. The keeper, whose name was Guhsciatazades (I shouldn't like to have to pronounce it, but you can only do your best, and make a dash for it), was grieved to the heart; he loved the holy old man, and venerated him. Now Simeon would not look at him, or even return his salute. Guhsciatazades went away, and, like another Peter, wept grievously. Then he bethought himself, and argued: If I am so grieved because a mere mortal is displeased with me, how shall I be able to bear the displeasure of God? So he repented, put on deep mourning, and came to sit as usual before the gate of the city.

Sapor II heard of the change in his favourite's looks and in his dress. He sent for him and asked him the cause. The keeper told him his story, how he had been doubly sinning: he had denied his God, and to keep his master's favour had pretended to adore the sun, a sin he abhorred. Sapor tried to shake his constancy, and bring him back to his former state of mind. But Guhsciatazades remained true to his Divine Master, and was beheaded for his faith. His last request was that Sapor would declare that the prisoner was dying, not for any crime, but for his faith; for the poor man wanted to make good the scandal he had given by his apostacy.

Sapor tried every means in his power to win over Simeon to his side, but to no purpose. So the decree went forth that he with his priests and people, a hundred at once, were to be beheaded. The whole band was assembled on the place of execution. Simeon was placed apart. His brethren were all to die before him. One by one they were brought to the block, and all died with courage and gladness. There was but one left, his name was Hananias. As he loosened his robe he was noticed to be trembling violently. An officer of the King, who had received many favours from his Sovereign, was moved with pity for the Christian, and, fearing lest he should lose his faith at the last moment, he cried out: "Hananias, banish all fear; shut your eyes one moment, and you will behold the light of Christ!" The young man closed his eyes. The axe fell, and he went happily to his Master.

A few moments after Hananias's death the venerable Simeon laid down his head and won his crown.

But Phasic, the Persian favourite, was doomed. He was hurried before Sapor and frankly confessed his words. Then he also proclaimed himself a Christian. Sapor, furious with the ungrateful man, as he called him, had him tortured to death in a manner too cruel to relate.

When we get to Heaven what a great many stories we shall hear! Think only of those 16,000 martyrs of Sapor's reign, and each of them with a story of his own. And they won't be boring stories, as some are in this world. They will all interest us, and we shall rejoice with everyone, for all tears will have been wiped from people's eyes, and they will know no more sorrow.

SCHOOLMASTERS

St. Anselm of Canterbury, April 21

O F COURSE, you are often asked, What will you be when you grow up? I suppose people ask little girls that nowadays. They used to ask boys only when I was young. But in these times little girls have to grow up into something, just as much as boys. Very soon, I suspect, they will grow into much more than the boys—that is, if the boys don't look after themselves, which no doubt they will.

I knew a boy who was asked this burning question: "What will you be wrhen you grow up?" "I'll be a schoolmaster, that I may beat the boys," he answered. Now, that was not very amiable of him, especially as he had never been beaten himself. And this makes me think of a schoolmaster who never beat his boys. He lived hundreds of years ago, when William the Conqueror was ruling in England. He was not an Englishman. He was born in Lombardy, at Aosta. He came to Bec, a monastery in the north of France, and there he taught the boys. And it was by gentleness and kindness that he won them; he did not punish nor did he scold much. There was no strap, or rod, or birch, or even an old slipper, which certainly is a very useful article of correction. Anselm had no instrument of punishment at all. Yet his boys learnt their lessons, were good, and well-behaved.

One day there came to see him a master from a neighbouring school. He listened to the classes at Bec. He saw the boys at play; he saw the work they did, and saw no woebegone face; he heard no groans, and he was astonished. He asked Anselm how he managed to make the boys so good without any punishment. His own were tiresome, incorrigible, wicked. So Anselm and his guest talked the matter over.

"We do our very best for them," the poor master said. "We beat them from morning till night, but I don't see any improvement." (How would you like that style of thing to be introduced ?)

"And how do they grow up?" Anselm asked.

"As dull and stupid as beasts!" the master answered.

"A famous system that must be," said Anselm, "if it changes men into beasts."

Then the monk told his companion how he tried kindness with his boys; how he was patient with them and loving; how he gave them liberty, and won their confidence little by little. Then the other master understood and went away, resolving to try this new method with his boys. I am sure I hope he did. But I hope, too, that his boys were worthy of being treated kindly. There may possibly be some natures that won't be good for kindness; then you have to try something else. But those are not the best natures, and I don't think there are many of them, thank God! Nobody could think much of a human being who had to be thrashed always before he did his duty, could they? It seems altogether the wrong way round. The will is guided by reason, and the reason is convinced by speech, not by blows, or ought to be. It must be a thick head that requires such arguments, and there is something wrong somewhere. Even a terrier can be taught to behave without the stick. It will shiver at a sharp word; a blow would crush its spirit. Well, I think a boy ought to have as much refinement as a terrier, if not more.

This St. Anselm, who was so kind to his scholars, was the great Archbishop of Canterbury who braved the fury of the Red King and King Henry I. The same who saw a hare escaping from the harriers. He watched the frightened thing, and as it came his way he forbade the dogs to touch it. It reminded him, he said, of a poor soul pursued by the devil. So the little hare got free, and I dare say it was better pleased than the hunters.

ST. GEORGE

April 23

O F COURSE, you think at once of a splendid soldier on horseback, with the dragon under his horse's feet; with the spear held high over its head, and aimed fatally at the scaly beast beneath. You think of England's war-cry, "St. George for Merry England!" You are proud of our national patron. You are not wrong with these high thoughts. England's patron is a splendid soldier, a grand figure in history, a hero who conquered a fierce dragon; for he was a Saint and a martyr. Let us see what is known about him.

George was born in Cappadocia, a province of Asia Minor. His parents were noble, and he was brought up to be a soldier. He was strong, rich, clever, and of winning manners. At that time Diocletian was Emperor; he became much attached to the young noble, and made him a tribune, which is much the same rank as colonel with us. From that moment George had a glorious career before him. He could rise easily in the State, for he was a royal favourite. But Diocletian was ill-advised, and issued wicked decrees against the Christians, and the most terrible persecution was set on foot. George threw up his commission, for he could not serve a master, he said, who persecuted God's Saints. Nor was George content to simply withdraw. He wrote to the Emperor and upbraided him for his impious conduct. For this offence George was seized and thrown into prison. There he was promised great things, threatened, and, when he remained constant, tortured. But all to no purpose. George was not a soldier for nothing. He fought a good fight and received the palm. On April 23 he was beheaded at Nicomedia.

The Greeks call St. George "the Great Martyr." In Constantinople there are six churches built in his honour. He is the patron of Genoa. Edward III instituted an order of knighthood in his honour; St. Gregory the Great reverenced him with peculiar devotion, so did Clotilda, wife of Clovis. With us his feast is kept as a day of devotion, though many, very many, Englishmen do not know whether there ever was a real Saint of the name. But you and I know there was, don't we?

Some of you are perhaps wondering why St. George is painted killing a dragon. Dragons like those we see in pictures there were certainly not in Diocletian's reign. So St. George could not have killed one. But the old writers and painters used to depict real monsters when they meant spiritual ones; and spiritual ones are truly the worst kind of monsters that ever you could see, or know, or fight with. St. George's monster was *human respect, love of the world*, which is worse than any dragon that ever was painted. Let us take this "Great Martyr" for our own particular patron, and ask him to help us fight our dragon, whatever it is, as bravely as he did.

ANIANUS, THE COBBLER

St. Anianus, Patriarch of Alexandria, April 25

THERE WAS a shoemaker who lived at Alexandria, that wonderful city of Egypt on the Nile. You must not suppose he made boots like ours. He lived in times far away from our own, when nobody wore such things; they wore sandals as children wear now. In those days nobody despised people who worked with their hands; it was thought an honourable thing to labour at a craft. So a shoemaker or a tent-maker, a tanner or a weaver, might be all honourable men; they might be learned and of good birth. There were snobs in those days, I don't doubt; but they were not precisely like the snobs of ours who turn up their noses at useful labour. Anianus was the man's name. He was good and just, but he did not know about Jesus Christ, and waited for someone to come and tell him the good tidings.

Anianus the cobbler was a Jew. He had heard strange rumours from the East of the advent of the Messiah, the long expected, Israel's promised Saviour. He had questioned all who had come over the borderland, or any who had crossed the Rhinocolura to tell him all they knew. And terrible things they told him—of the short, bright passage of the Wonder-Worker of Nazareth, of His shameful death, of His much-talked-of Resurrection; of the bold preaching of His fishermen disciples, of their being persecuted, and of their deaths in distant countries.

Anianus listened and thought much. The story was fascinating, if only it were true.

One day there was a press of work in Anianus's shop, and he bent over his leather till the perspiration flowed down his cheeks, and his hands trembled. By an awkward movement he ran the awl into his hand, and made an ugly wound. Faint and sick, he sank on to his bench, whilst he let the blood fall from the wound, too helpless to bind it up.

At that moment a stranger entered the booth, and seeing what had happened hastened to the man's relief. He took the bleeding hand in his left, and with his right made the sign as of a cross over it, and said some words in a foreign tongue. The blood ceased to flow, the wound closed, and the rough palm was unscarred. Anianus looked up into the stranger's face. There was on it that look of peace and calm that is seen upon the face of some holy people. The stranger spoke first, for Anianus was too bewildered even to thank him. His name, he said, was Mark, John Mark, for he was a Hebrew by birth and a Christian by religion. Then the face of Anianus brightened. Here was one who could tell him of what he had so longed to know—all about that Christ of whom the travellers spoke; of His work upon earth, of the Church He was to found. So the two sat together, and the press of work was forgotten, and the time for meals passed, and neither was hungry; and the night came, and still both sat sleepless there. For Mark had much to tell. It was he who had heard from the great St. Peter all about the dear Lord's life and death, of the miracles He had wrought, of the wisdom that dwelt upon His lips, of the loving-kindness that came from His hands. He heard of His death and of His glorious Resurrection, of the fearful prophecy that had come true, of the destruction of Jerusalem and dispersion of God's favoured nation, of the Gentiles who were drinking in the glad tidings as a child drinks in its sweet milk. And if Mark loved to tell, Anianus loved to listen.

That day Anianus became a Christian, and from that day worked for his new-found Lord with all his strength. He learnt the truths of Christianity with so much ease that Mark made him a Bishop, and for four years they worked the diocese together. They visited the churches, they taught the ignorant, and served the sick. And when Mark was obliged to quit Alexandria he left his friend behind to govern in his place. So for eighteen years Anianus the shoemaker was Bishop of the great city of Alexandria. "He was a man well pleasing to God and admirable in all things," says a

great Christian historian. And this is nice to think of:
the two great friends and Saints, Mark and Anianus,
have their feast-day kept together on April 25.

THE CASK OF ST. CATHERINE

St. Catherine of Siena, April 30

IT WAS a cask of the very best wine, and Giacomo Benincasa had forbidden anyone in the house to use it without his express permission. One day he sent for a flagon from the cellar. The messenger came back with a startled look on his face. The cask was empty, he said. The whole family was in a stir. Who could have taken the wine? Who had dared to disobey the master's orders? Catherine was in her little room; she heard the noise and the voices. And she knew the answer to the questions. She had taken the wine. For she had heard it was of superior quality, and, as was her wont, she had given it as the best to God's poor. So she left her prayers, and went straight to her father. "Dear father, why are you troubled?" she said. "Do not worry. I will go and draw the wine." She went, and, kneeling down by the empty cask, prayed to Our Lord: "O Lord, Thou knowest that this wine has been spent in Thy honour and glory for the needs of the poor, therefore do not permit that the lack of it should be a scandal to my father and the family." Then she made the sign of the cross over the cask, and the wine flowed abundantly.

From the day when the wine flowed from the empty cask, it came to be a saying in Siena when anything appeared to be inexhaustible, that it was like St. Catherine's cask. This Catherine was the wonderful St. Catherine of Siena, who advised Popes and Kings and Queens.

Another cask was just as miraculous. Good Bonincasa had given his best-loved daughter leave to give whatever she liked to the poor. So she drew freely from the wine that was used daily by the family. It ought by rights to have served the family twenty days at most; but at the end of a month the cask was as full as at the beginning. Month after month passed, and still the barrel showed no signs of being empty. It was only when the summer was over and the vintage at hand that the cask ran dry enough to be used for a new wine. Now this wonder was worked because the Saint loved the poor and trusted in God. You have to do both, and then things come right.

But this was easy charity, you may think. Listen to this, then:

In the hospital there was a poor woman whose case was declared to be leprosy. Do you know what that is? The most deadly and frightful of all diseases, and the most catching. Catherine heard that the poor creature was to be isolated, but as she offered to come every day to dress her wounds and tend her, the invalid was allowed to remain. Never did a day go by but Catherine was at the woman's bedside, cheerful and tender, washing, dressing, soothing the afflicted leper. You would naturally suppose that Cecca would be most grateful and humble. Not at all. She expected everything as a right; she resented the least delay, mocked at her benefactress, grumbled, insulted her. But not one word of complaint ever crossed the Saint's lips, so that in the end Cecca herself marvelled. But Lapa, Catherine's mother, came very near forbidding her daughter to continue her work, for she feared, as well she might, that Catherine herself would contract the disease. Catherine, however, was not in the least anxious. It mattered little to her whether she was a leper or not, so long as God's poor were relieved. And, as if to try her faith to the utmost, Catherine's hands were one day found to be leprous! Horror seized upon all. Those who had praised her charity most, now blamed her imprudence and avoided her company. Catherine was unmoved. She continued her kind offices, though the illness lasted a very long time. And when at last Cecca died, Catherine was true to her charge to the very end. But when the last sod of earth was thrown by Catherine on the leper's body, her hands were restored to health, and became whiter than any other part of her body. You see Our Lord is never outdone in generosity.

ASH WEDNESDAY

O F ALL the stories of the Old Testament, that of Jonas and the conversion of Nineve is the most wonderful. The great, prosperous, heathen capital of Assyria stood out amongst the cities of the earth as one whose wickedness came up before God. Its destruction was at hand; yet one more warning was to be given to it. Jonas was to preach a Divine threat in its thoroughfares: "Yet forty days and Nineve shall be destroyed." And for three days the Prophet proclaimed the terrible truth. And the men of Nineve believed in God; and they proclaimed a fast, and put on sackcloth, from the greatest to the least. And the word came to the King of Nineve; and he rose up out of his throne, and cast away his robe from him, and was clothed with sackcloth and sat in ashes. And he caused it to be proclaimed and published in Nineve from the mouth of the King and the Princes, saying: "Let neither man nor beast, oxen nor sheep taste anything; let them not feed nor taste water. And let men and beasts be covered with sackcloth and cry to the Lord with all their strength; and let them turn from their evil ways and from the iniquity that is on their hands. Who can tell if God will turn away from His fierce anger and we shall not perish?" This was no exterior conversion, no outward semblance of penance and humiliation. "God is not mocked." He sees the heart, and the heart of the Ninevites must have been truly contrite, truly humble; for "God saw their works that they were turned from their evil ways and God had mercy regarding the evil which He said that He would do to them and He did it not." Such was the effect of a call to penance upon a pagan, sensual people; and such was its power with God that it stayed His avenging hand.

The three Sundays Septuagesima, Sexagesima, and Quinquagesima, bring us by easy steps within sight of Lent, the Church's time for penance and fasting and prayer. "Yet forty days!" is the cry. How are we going to listen to the warning voice?

"But we are not pagans," we may say; "our wickedness does not go up before the Lord like that of the Assyrians. What was good for the wicked is not a proved good for us." The answer is, penance is good for the holy as well as for the sinful; it preserves as well as atones. Saints have felt the need of it in all ages and at all times, at the beginning of their conversion and at the end of their lives. In whichever category, therefore, we may think well to place ourselves—Saint or sinner— penance is necessary for us; and we know it well. We are not true to our best nature when we deny the need of mortification; for we feel the conflict within us, the struggle between the good and the bad. We know the good should conquer, and that it cannot conquer without pain and that that pain is mortification in one form or another.

Why do we dread penance? Because it opposes our lower nature; in simple terms, because it hurts. Nature shrinks from what hurts; yet it is astonishing how soon penance becomes easy when it is undertaken with courage. Courage counts as two-thirds of the necessary outfit for any undertaking, supernatural or natural. What we have to do, then, is to brace ourselves up to look forward bravely, and suffer magnanimously all the little mortifications proposed by the Church as to fasting, abstinence, and prayer. They are few enough as it is; far be it from us to wish them fewer or less binding.

Above all, let us remember that whatever exemptions we may justly plead, we cannot justly exempt ourselves from the spirit of penance during Lent. We must feel its pressure, come under its discipline. The very weakness or labour that keeps us from fasting may itself be our penance, if suffered in the right spirit.

Now, is this determination to spend the forty days of Lent in the spirit of the Church going to make us sad and long-faced? God forbid! We might as well be Pharisees at once. If mortification does not bring with it cheerfulness and holy joy there is something wrong with it, and we had better find out what it is as soon as possible. No. The most mortified are the most cheerful. Those shiver most who bathe at the edge of the sea and get wet by dribblets; those who plunge in deep are in a glow before they feel the shock; those who do penance grudgingly do not taste its joy.

Dare I try to be amongst the cheerful givers, the generous sufferers? Yes, because the "love of Jesus urgeth me."

"OH, COME AND MOURN
WITH ME AWHILE!"

Y
OU KNOW why I have written those words, don't
you? And you know what they mean. I don't
think we could bear to read of anything but Our
Blessed Lord in Holy Week. The Church is mourning
for Him "as the manner is to mourn for an only son."
We should not like to be the only ones to seem not
to care.

I was thinking, therefore, if I wrote down for
each day in Holy Week what Our Lord is generally
supposed to have done and suffered on that day, it
might help you to spend it with Him, and make the
services of the Church easier to follow. There is only
one week in a year given up to the Sacred Passion.
I think, then, we ought to try and suffer with Our
Lord the whole of that little time. People with pains
and sorrows often spend the whole year grieving over
those aches and pains and telling others about them.
Our Blessed Lord hardly ever spoke of His sufferings,
and when He did, it was for the sake of others, to
prepare them for the terrible trials that were near at

hand. Now I will tell you what it is supposed Our Saviour did on these coming holy days.

PALM SUNDAY.

Jesus enters Jerusalem in triumph. His disciples have put Him on a colt; they have strewn their garments on the way; they have cut branches and waved them; they have sung hosannas in His honour. Jesus bears with their enthusiasm, just as He will bear with their perfidy. He lets them lead in joy; very soon, He knows, they will pace the same streets in anger, and will hoot and jeer.

MONDAY.

The chief priests assemble together. Their jealousy of Our Lord has come to a dreadful pass. They have determined to take His life, and they look out for someone who will help them to seize Him without any disturbance. Jesus goes in and out of Jerusalem, knowing their wicked plots, yet taking no precautions; for He is going to give up His life, they are not going to take it from Him. He is to be seen in the Temple, healing the sick, instructing everyone. When night comes He goes to the little village of Bethany, where His friends, Lazarus and Martha and Mary, receive Him, though they endanger their lives by their hospitality.

TUESDAY.

Our Lord has much to say to His people. He is soon to leave them, but He wants to tell them many things.

He teaches in parables, and He works miracles; He receives all who want to see Him; He blames the wicked Scribes and Pharisees; He warns the people to beware of them and their doctrines. As He is sitting in the grand hall of the Temple He sees a poor widow come up and drop her mite into one of the brazen trumpets. Jesus loves her for her act, and praises her before all the people. "This poor widow has cast more than they all into the treasury. For all they did cast in of their abundance; but she of her want cast in all that she had, even her whole living." That night Jesus was anointed with a most precious ointment by Mary, the sinner.

WEDNESDAY.

See Judas making his way to the house of the chief priests. He has got away secretly. The other disciples do not know that he is gone; he goes straight forward, up the steep streets, past the houses of the great, till he comes to the one where a secret council is sitting. He is expected. Our Lord's enemies know something of this man; they have hoped that it would be he who would help them in their plot. The door opens and the man enters. His head hangs, his face is white. He says, without looking up: "What will you give me, and I will deliver Him unto you?" And they were glad, and covenanted to give him thirty pieces of silver. And he promised. Look at the traitor for one moment: see his face, the movement of his restless hands, the twitching of his lip, the shifting of his feet; see him take the pieces of silver and turn to go. Was his sin worth the reward? Is sin ever worth its reward?

MAUNDY THURSDAY.

Jesus is in the upper room. His face has a look of wonderful love. He says to the Apostles: "With desire I have desired to eat this Pasch with you." All preparations have been made. The Twelve are with Him in the decorated supper-room. The wine is on the table, the wheaten bread is ready; it serves first for the Jewish feast, then for the new Christian banquet. Our Lord consecrates the bread and wine; they become His Sacred Body and Blood, the Food of our soul and the Pledge of eternal salvation. When the supper is over, and Our Lord leads the way to the Garden of Gethsemane, He falls into an agony "and prays the longer." Judas comes and gives Him the traitor's kiss, and the soldiers lead Him off, because His time has come. He wills to die for love of us.

"O ALL YOU THAT PASS BY THE WAY!"

"SUPPOSE!" How often we say that; or, "Let us pretend!" And then we imagine all sorts of things. We are kings or princes, knights or ladies of high degree; we live in castles or in sunny cottages, or in log-cabins in settlements. And we pretend so well that we forget the pretending and feel real.

I want to do some pretending this week, but sad, sad pretending, and doubly sad because my pretending will not be half so sad as the reality. I want to go back in time some nineteen hundred years; in space some hundreds of miles to the Near East, to the Holy Land, to the City of Jerusalem. I want to spend the time with Mary, the Mother of Jesus, and try to feel as she felt when the stone was rolled across the sepulchre, and the sun set on Calvary that Friday, the first to be called "Good."

And I want you all to come too. Could we talk today of anything but Jesus suffering? Could we stand this week anywhere but on Calvary? If our hearts are hard and we do not share Our Lord's pain, and our eyes have tears only for our own griefs, let us turn to Mary and ask her to soften our nature and teach us better things.

> "O thou Mother, fount of Love,
> Touch my spirit from above,
>   Make my heart with thine accord.

> "Make me feel as thou hast felt,
> Make my soul to glow and melt
>   With the love of Christ my Lord.

> "Holy Mother! pierce me through,
> In my heart each wound renew
>   Of my Saviour crucified.

> "Let me share with thee His pain
> Who for all my sins was slain,
>   Who for me in torments died.

> "Let me mingle tears with thee,
> Mourning Him Who mourned for me,
>   All the days that I may live."

Suppose we are standing in a narrow street of Jerusalem. It is early morning, but there is much going and coming. It is Paschal Week, and Jerusalem is crowded; but the excitement is more than festive. There is agitation in the air. Men pass us by whose faces are lined with passion, lines which have been written by cunning and cruelty, rage and cowardly fear. Evidently there is to be some spectacle. People are taking their stand in the street, choosing good points of view, filling the balconies, peering through the embrasures. We will stand by too, and watch. It is the third hour; the crowd increases; something is coming; there is a yelling, a shouting, and hooting. We ask what it can be.

The answer is: Jesus of Nazareth has been condemned; nobody exactly knows why, but it must be all right. The chief priests have judged the case. A man near us asks, what is the sentence? "Crucifixion," is the short answer, to which is added, "on Calvary." The air gets stifling as the mass of men rolls forward.

The Roman ensign is in sight now; the Centurion's plume floats on the breeze; the spears of the soldiers gleam. There are the criminals. The first is a brutal-looking man with dark hair hanging over his shoulders. The Second! we cannot see Him. Between Him and us there comes the veiled figure of a stately woman; she stretches out her hands; she is very pale and quite speechless. But words are not needed. Thirty years of life and love have passed between that Mother and Son. The meeting takes but a moment of time. Blows are showered upon the Man and He passes out of sight, beyond the bend in the way. Mary is drawn back by a trembling hand, and the dreadful procession passes onwards.

We press with the crowd to Calvary. An unbroken stream of humanity stretches from the city to the place of execution. We are dragged on, willingly or not.

When we arrive Jesus has been hoisted on to His Cross and hangs between two thieves, who shout across to each other, reviling and cursing. Under the feet of Jesus of Nazareth there stands a little group of loving friends. We recognize the youth John, the sinner Magdalen, the Mother Mary.

"At the Cross her station keeping,
  Stood the mournful Mother weeping,
    Close to Jesus to the last.

"Through her heart, His sorrow sharing,
  All His bitter anguish bearing,
    Now at length the sword has passed.

"Oh, how sad and sore distressed
  Was that Mother highly blest
    Of the sole begotten One!

"Christ above in torments hangs,
  She beneath beholds the pangs
    Of her dying glorious Son."

Let us stand here too, children, and hear and see again the things that took place on that hillock nineteen hundred years ago. Let us put aside the daily thoughts of life for a little while and for these next few days bear the mournful Mother company.

"Is there one who would not weep,
  Whelm'd in miseries so deep,
    Christ's dear Mother to behold?

"Can the human heart refrain
  From partaking in that pain,
    In that Mother's pain untold?

"Bruised, derided, cursed, defiled,
  She beheld her tender Child,
    All with bloody scourges rent.

"For the sins of His own nation,
  Saw Him hang in desolation
    Till His spirit forth He sent."

O all you that pass by the Way

EASTERTIDE

JESUS was dead. Joseph of Arimathea and Nicodemus had come to the burying. They were rich men and well-known as city councillors. The sacred body had been handed over to them, and they had "wrapped it up in a clean linen cloth and laid it in a new monument which had been hewed out of the rock," and a great round stone had been rolled to the door of the monument. Darkness was fast coming on; Mary and John and Magdalen had gone home; the crowd had dispersed; the midday darkness had been lifted; there was a mysterious stillness in the air. In Jerusalem there was a hurrying to and fro, for the Sabbath was at hand and all work must be got through before sunset. The Sanhedrin party had triumphed and was glad. Pilate was sullen and uneasy; he had given in against reason, justice, and conscience. Still, with all their triumph, the chief priests were not at rest. They had heard rumours of a Resurrection, and a final and glorious triumph; they must take effective measures to prevent the possibility of such an event. So, with Pilate's leave—who is so sick of their intrigues that he would have granted anything—they station a guard round the sepulchre: men paid to watch night and day to prevent the Apostles from coming and stealing the body. Poor Apostles! they were thinking of hiding themselves, not of defying the Sanhedrin. Peter had denied his Master; Judas had betrayed Him; the eight had left Him in the hands of His enemies. And the stone was made fast, and sealed with the great Sanhedrin seal.

As the first day of the week dawns, three stately figures are seen moving through the garden, making straight for the new sepulchre. Mary Magdalen, Mary of James, and Mary of Salome are bearing sweet spices to finish the Master's burying, too hastily performed on the sad Friday's eve. They expect to find the body where they had seen it; they had noted the exact position, that there might be no delay or difficulty. Of course there would be the great stone to be rolled back, but that was not a serious matter. As they approach they find the stone gone and the sepulchre open. They enter and see "a young man sitting on the right side clothed with a white robe, and they were astonished." The Angel tells them gently that they have nothing to fear. Jesus is risen. They must go and tell His disciples; they must spread the glorious news and gladden the sad hearts on that great first day, the first of the new era, the first day of rest.

But when did Jesus rise? And how? And who was there to see? Between sunset and sunrise Jesus rose— by His own infinite power—with no mortal eye to see or human mouth to tell. Silently, in the dead of night, He burst the bonds of death and raised His blessed body to glorious life again. Jesus died in shame before thousands. He rose in triumph when none were by.

Just think, children, of His power, the strong guard, the sealed stone, death itself—all overcome by His mere will. He laid down His life and He took it up again. Life and death are in His hands.

And this is *our* Redeemer, *our* Leader! This is He in Whom we place our trust, the One Who has promised to save us, Who has the will and the power. Won't you trust Him, and won't you be proud of Him?

TOWARDS EVENING

THE GREAT Feast of the Pasch was over, and the busy week had begun again. Jerusalem was crowded with strangers from all parts of the world; many were preparing to return home, and were forming caravans just outside the city; others were still lingering in the Holy City, hearing and discussing the wonderful events of the last few days. Our Blessed Lady had adored her Divine Son in His risen body, and He had filled her heart with gladness and wonderful peace. The Apostles were full of amazement at the stories that were being circulated concerning the Resurrection; some believed, but some doubted, and thought the holy women had been deceived by their overwrought nerves. Two men, full of doubt and restlessness, left the Holy City and turned for an evening walk to the northwest, to a little village about seven miles distant. They were weary of talking and wondering; they wanted to get right away from sights and scenes that were full of sorrow.

As they walked and talked about Our Lord, a Stranger came up to them and joined Himself to their company. "What are these discourses that you hold

one with another, and are sad?" He asked. A look at
their faces was enough to show that something was
amiss; but this Stranger read hearts. The men turned
upon Him astonished. He had come from Jerusalem
and did not know what all were talking about. "Art
thou only a stranger in Jerusalem, and hast not known
the things that have been done there in these days?"
Cleophas answered. "What things?" their Companion
asked. Then their mouths were opened, and in glowing
words they spoke of their dead Master, "one mighty in
word and work before God and all in the people." He
was a Prophet, they said, in Whom all Israel hoped;
but He was dead, and they were sad and troubled. The
Stranger listened patiently till all the sad tale of doubt
and fear and cowardice was told; then, with a tender
look at the two, He upbraided them for want of faith:
"O foolish and slow of heart to believe in all things
which the Prophets have spoken. Ought not Christ
to have suffered these things and so to enter into His
glory?" The three were passing through rocky country,
stepping westward as the sun was setting. Before them,
in the far distance, lay the land of Samaria, behind the
hills of Judea. A little speck at the end of the white,
winding road was Emmaus, its rounded roofs shining
in the red sun. The Stranger spoke all the time. He
went over the history of their nation they knew so
well, but yet understood so badly. He showed them
how the prophecies had been fulfilled by the very
death and shame that had shaken their faith. The men

listened with bent head and rapt attention. But the Stranger saw the gates of the town were near at hand; He did not intend to go in. "He made as if He would go farther." But the action roused them; they begged Him, and almost by compulsion managed to keep Him with them. All three entered a little inn. The meal began; they asked their Guest to break bread and give the blessing. He took it in His venerable hands and looked up to Heaven. Instantly they knew Him—Jesus their Master, their Lord, risen as the Prophets had said; then he vanished from their sight. He had done His work, He had comforted them, strengthened and enlightened them; then He left them. "Was not our heart burning within us," they say to each other, "whilst He spoke in the way, and opened to us the Scriptures?"

So that was the way the two disciples spent their Easter Sunday, walking with Our Lord Jesus Christ, with their hearts aglow with His love. Are they not to be envied? And would not you and I like to have been with them? I wish you all every Easter blessing and the greatest of all blessings, the personal love of Our Lord.

THE SPIRIT OF OUR RISEN LORD

I READ a little time ago in a book* that some day I hope you will read yourselves, a legend called "The Bag of Sand." It has not one word about the Resurrection of Our Blessed Lord, but it made me think of Him at once. Let me tell you the legend; I think you will see what I mean.

Once, a long time ago, in a monastery far away, a monk, who had long lived a holy life, but who had grown careless with age, committed a crime. We are not told what the sin was, but it filled the hearts of all the Fathers and Brothers with deepest grief. The sinner had been parted from the rest of his brethren, and was waiting, in remorse and solitude, for the sentence to be passed upon him; but the sentence was no easy thing to pass, for there were many things to be considered. There was the poor sinner himself; there were the brethren of the monastery; there was the disedification abroad. So the Fathers sat in council and heard opinions as they were uttered. "Dismiss him," said a severe disciplinarian; "he is not worthy

---
* "The Hidden Servants," by F. Alexander.

to remain among us." "Imprison him for life," said another, with quivering lip. "Let him labour long and hard, and give him his food and dwelling apart," said a gentler nature. But the Abbot shook his head, and with wistful eyes watched the door, for a holy hermit had been called from a far-away cell to come and help to decide this momentous question. He was known as holy—inspired, some said; he was older and wiser than any present at the council; he would bring words of wisdom.

So the Fathers watched his coming. And when one keen-eyed youth saw the dim figure in the distance, all arose and went to meet him. But why was his step so slow? Why did he stop so often as if weary with carrying? Weary with carrying he was. Upon his shoulders he bore a heavy burden. Eagerly the monks stepped towards him and begged to ease him of his load. But the old man shook his head, saying, with downcast eyes, "These are my sins, dear brother; I must bear them with me when I come to judge a fellow brother." Then the Abbot raised the burden from the bowed shoulders, opened the heavy bag, and—found it filled with finest sand. As the holy men drew near and saw the contents of the sack, a great hush fell upon them all; their own sins came to their minds, and they felt that, were they all numbered, greater even than grains of sand would their number be. The Abbot spoke: "God alone must judge us all!" he said. The assembly broke up. Some went to find the sorrowing brother, some to thank God for His mercy. That evening the poor sinner was found praying in the chapel with the rest.

Now, can you tell me why this legend made me think of our risen Lord? That Father-hermit, who had lived nearest to God and was dearest to Him, had only words of loving-kindness and forgiveness upon his tongue. Do you remember, when Our Lord came among His own after His Resurrection, how He treated the Apostles? They had fled from Him in His shame and sorrow; Peter had denied Him; all had doubted His prophecies; all had lost hope in the cause. But not one word of reproach did Our Lord utter. For his threefold denial, the only penance enjoined on Peter is a threefold act of love. Jesus waits patiently for returning faith in His disciples; He heaps proof upon proof; He allows the doubting Apostle Thomas to touch the wounds of His hands and put in his hand into the open side, and when at last Thomas cries out: "My Lord and my God!" Jesus answers gently: "Because thou hast seen Me, Thomas, thou hast believed. Blessed are they who believe without seeing!" He calls the disciples going to Emmaus "foolish and slow of heart." But they did not even understand that there was any reproach in the words, for when Our Lord had disappeared, they said to one another: "Was not our heart glowing within us as He spoke upon the way!" Glowing with love and faith and hope and happiness, that is.

This is why the dear old hermit, with his precious bag of sand, reminds me of our dear Lord. He brings with Him love and forgiveness and *forgetfulness* for all. Denial, cowardice, hopelessness—all is forgotten and forgiven. Let us, at this blessed Easter-time, see if our dispositions are like these. Are we well with everyone? Have we wiped out old scores and made a clean sweep of grievances? Have we a humble heart full of charity, like the dear old hermit and—like, in our small way— our own dear risen Saviour?

ARMS AND ARMOUR

Don't you like playing at soldiers? The children in my street like it. There were three of them yesterday, one was captain, and two were privates. They had wooden swords and paper belts; but they were very earnest, the captain especially. He was about six; the others were not more than five. I was glad their swords were only wood. The captain gave peremptory, but rather confused, orders, and when the men did not obey, he shoved them about or hit them with the naked blade.

There is a fascination about a soldier. We think of him as a man who is prepared to die at any moment, to sell his life dearly to his foe, but give it freely for his country; so we start at the sound of a drum and leave our work and follow with our eye the sturdy fellows as they tramp past.

Yes, the soldier is a useful man, and so the King has them housed and fed and armed at the country's expense. They are to be provided with all that is necessary in peace and war, but particularly in war. The best and most up-to-date of arms are put into their hands; they are not stinted for powder or shot;

millions are spent on their outfit and their transport. Everything that will make resistance easy is procured for them, because they are the soldiers of the King and have to fight for him.

The Church tells us that we are to be soldiers of a King. She waits till a little baptized child comes to the use of reason, then she invites him to confess his sins; she feeds him with Heavenly Bread to nourish his soul. So far her little charge is a child in his father's house, a sheltered and protected little one. His passions are scarcely rebels as yet; they have not declared war and sent out the battle shout. But the boy grows and strengthens. He meets a threefold foe, and has to fight. The Church is ready then. She has strength for him—arms and armour. She comes with the Sacrament that makes him a strong and perfect Christian and a soldier of Jesus Christ.

She lifts up her champion's forehead and signs it with the sign of the Cross; she anoints his brow with the most sacred oil; she spreads her hands twice over his head, and calls upon the Paraclete, the Comforter, to descend and take possession, to strengthen and console. Then her son is a soldier, a knight, even, in the great King's service; he is promoted, raised from the ranks, set apart. He has to fight a good fight, so the Church bestows upon him her richest gifts.

Two special needs has man: light to know, strength to do. The Holy Ghost in Confirmation brings both. He has four gifts for man's mind: *Wisdom*, that savours

Divine things; *Understanding*, that grasps truth; *Counsel*, that distinguishes the path to tread; and *Knowledge*, that turns all known facts into helps to Heaven. For the will there are three precious gifts: *Fortitude*, that gives strength to stand for the right; *Piety*, that keeps the heart tender towards the Heavenly Father; *Fear of the Lord*, that awes it into filial reverence.

There were grown-up men once who were slow to understand, selfish, and proud—cowards even. They quarrelled amongst themselves; they wanted best places; they fled and deserted their Master. But these were confirmed, they received the Holy Ghost, and they became soldiers of the King, Apostles and martyrs.

And remember, Confirmation has not lost its power. The Sacraments always give grace to those who receive them worthily. Their power does not rise and fall according to the century. Confirmation in the twentieth century is the same as in the first. The Holy Ghost descends upon us as He did upon the Twelve and those with them in the upper room.

So go forth and receive this blessed Sacrament with all the fervour of your young hearts. Strengthen your faith to believe in the great Giver of gifts. Stir up your hope to expect all good things, and inflame your hearts to love Him with a deep, fervent love.

> "All glory to the Father be,
>   With His co-equal Son,
> The same to Thee, great Paraclete,
>   While endless ages run."

THE FEAST OF CORPUS CHRISTI

Thursday after the Octave of Pentecost

THE TITLE means the Feast of the Body of Christ. What great mysteries are contained in these few words! A bigoted onlooker sees us Catholics kneel before the statue of Our Lady, of St. Joseph, or a patron Saint, and he sees us kneel before the Blessed Sacrament. To him the acts are the same, and both idolatry. It is true outwardly they are the same—the knee is bent in each case; but look into the heart, question the mind, and see the difference. The genuflection before the image of Our Lady is humble supplication, childlike reverence; before the Blessed Sacrament it is adoration, and means supreme worship. Then what is the Blessed Sacrament, that It causes such a difference in intention?

It is the Body of Christ. To an instructed Catholic all is said. By the hypostatic union the Godhead dwells in the Sacred Body. The Divinity is there, and the Humanity of "the Son of man." The Body of Christ—a part put for the whole—is the Blessed Sacrament of the altar, that great gift Our Lord bestowed upon the Church on the eve of His Passion. "I will not leave you orphans," He had promised, and to fulfil His word He came to dwell amongst us, content with anything so that He might be with us, be of use to us, within reach of the poor, the loving, the sick.

"*Who* is the Blessed Sacrament?" the child asked. St. Philip's answer will serve our purpose: "Come and see!" We look the world over in our mind's eye; we trace Our Lord's dwelling-places, guided by the little glimmering light. It shines sometimes in stately churches, in splendid cathedrals, but very seldom; in warehouses, barns, garrets, caves, wherever man can make room for the Lord of Majesty, wherever the creature can make shift to do with his Creator, and here very often. We look for His associates; we find some learned, some rich, some renowned. But these are few; they are mostly too busy to have time to spare for the "Wisdom of the Father." We find, however, the poor, workmen and women, labourers from the field, factory hands, and children—these sing His praises, lisp their prayers, and admire the beauty of His poor house. We ask about His duties. We find a "clean oblation" is offered "from the rising to the setting of the sun"; the hungry are fed—line after line of craving souls come for their daily bread; the sick strengthened for the Homeward journey; the sorrowful listened to with patient silence, the doubtful counselled, the perplexed enlightened, the broken-hearted soothed and comforted.

Can we answer the child's question now: "Who is the Blessed Sacrament?" Do not these haunts, these associates, these duties, point out Jesus of Nazareth, the Healer of the sick, the Comfort of the afflicted, the Companion of the outcast, the Victim of the Cross? It is true His way of working now is different. In the Temple, in the streets of Nazareth, in the fields of Galilee, and on the rugged hills of Judea, Jesus spoke and touched, wrought miracles on nature and upon disease; but His working was not more real then than now. More hungry are fed now every day with miraculous Bread than upon Galilee's shore. More sick are strengthened with the Food of the Way than ever in the land of Palestine. Then there was one Bleeding Victim on Calvary's Mount; now, on the altar, there is offered thousands of times a day that clean oblation promised of old.

Yes, Jesus of Nazareth is the Blessed Sacrament. Ask the child on its First Communion day, the priest after his first Mass, the dying man after Viaticum. They will tell you they have felt the sweetness of His words, they have felt a joy within them and a gladness that could only come from One, a God-made man, the Divine Lover of souls.

"I have Jesus within me," a child said. "He is taking care of me, and I am taking care of Him." This was the afternoon of the boy's First Communion day. Jesus has taken care of us all the days that we have lived. Is it not our turn to take care of Him, to honour Him? Will not our hearts go out to Him at least on this great Feast of His? Shall we not visit Him, bring

Him flowers and candles? Better still, bring our hearts brimful of love and gratitude and adoration? "Lord, where dwellest Thou?" the first Apostles asked. We know where He dwells. But to us as to them comes Our Lord's answer: "Come and see!" We will come and see today. And so lovingly will we come, and with such lively faith, that we shall be led to repeat the visit often, and still more often, until we are one of those to whom the Presence of Our Lord in His Sacrament is life and hope and gladness.

> "O Sacrament most holy, O Sacrament Divine,
> All praise and all thanksgiving be every moment Thine."

B.THOMAS MORE

MAY

B.JOHN FISHER

MARTYRS OF ENGLAND

May 4

I F EVER a time comes when you want strength above your own to practise your faith, courage to profess it, love to cherish it, pray to Blessed Thomas More, ex-Chancellor of England, the keenest wit of his age, the most learned lawyer, the most upright courtier, the most loving father and husband, the most loyal son of the Church.

Once upon a time young King Henry VIII might have been seen with his arm round his Chancellor's neck, laughing at his jest, admiring his deep learning. But again, once on a time, Henry might have been seen signing the death-warrant of his ex-Chancellor, because he would not swear that Henry, false to God and man, was head of the Church in England, and that his marriage with Anne Boleyn was lawful.

More was confined in the Tower, and with him, nearer to his death by fifteen days, was the venerable Cardinal Fisher. After some months of solitary imprisonment, More was gladdened by the visits of Margaret, his best-loved daughter. Margaret found her father chastened by the Cross; a supernatural beauty ennobled his dear face; he was as playful as ever, but there were added an earnestness and depth that had hardly been his before. Though these precious visits were short, father and daughter knelt down together and recited the Litany and the seven penitential Psalms. Then they poured forth their whole soul to each other. Once More said, to comfort her when she was sad: "They that put me here, Meg, ween, as I verily believe, that they have done me a high displeasure; but I assure thee, my own good daughter, had it not been for wife and children, I would long ere this have chosen a straighter cell."

After a grave discussion, the martyr said gently: "Meg, though it soundeth like a riddle, there is a case where a man may lose his head and yet have no harm. I have not in this matter forgotten the counsel of Our Lord in the Gospel, that we should count the cost ere we begin to build. Full many a restless night, Margaret, while my wife slept, have I weighed and counted, ere yet I closed my eyes, what peril might befall me; and I am sure no care came heavier than mine. In thinking of it I often had a right heavy heart; but yet I thank my Lord that for all that I never thought to change."

See how human the martyrs were! They felt loss and separation just as we do, but they knew they must suffer even death itself for the love of God and their faith.

Bishop Fisher, in his seventy-seventh year, was sentenced to death, and was beheaded on June 21. "Dost thou not mark it is our marriage day?" he cried as he dressed himself with scrupulous care to ascend the scaffold. Blessed Thomas More followed him there on July 6. On the eve he wrote with a coal his last letter to his daughter, sending, through her, messages to each of the family. "To-morrow is St. Thomas's Eve, and tomorrow I long to go to God. It were a day meet and convenient to me."

This he said because he felt his devotion to St. Thomas of Canterbury doubled just then, as he was dying for so nearly the same cause, and was to keep one and the same feast-day. On the scaffold joy broke out in the martyr's words. After he had said the whole of the *Miserere* Psalm, he kissed the executioner, who was woefully downhearted. He told him to pluck up his spirit and be a man, adding: "My neck is very short; see, therefore, thou strike not awry to save thy credit." Thus did Blessed Thomas More go to the God he loved and served with his whole heart and soul, and strength, and mind. Oh, children, pray that you and I may live and die as confessors of that Faith for which the martyrs Fisher and More died!

THE PRICE OF A SECRET

St. John Nepomucene, May 16

Tʜᴇʀᴇ are some children who are afraid to go to Confession. They get all sorts of strange ideas into their heads. These ideas don't come from God. They come from our own defects of character sometimes, and sometimes from the devil. If we are uncharitable, we think the confessor will be wanting in charity towards us. If we are impatient, we think the confessor will snub us as we snub others. If we can't keep a secret, we imagine that the priest can't keep one either, and that our sins will be made known to anyone. The devil helps to our discomfort, of course, too. He makes us feel far more shame after the sins are committed than before. Confession before we sin seems so very easy, whilst after the sin our cheeks burn and our eyes are full of tears at the very thought of it.

Perhaps of all the troubles with some children that of the *secret* is the worst. They cannot believe that the sins they confess are buried for ever and ever; that the priest cannot, and will not, ever reveal them; that there is a special providence that guards the tongue of the priest. Now for little children who are worried with such silly thoughts as these, I am going to tell the story of what it cost one holy priest to keep the seal of Confession unbroken. And remember it has never been proved that in all the millions of confessions that have been made since Confession was instituted, one of these was ever made known.

Long ago, in the fourteenth century, there lived a great Empress, Jane, daughter of Albert of Bavaria and wife of Wenceslaus, Emperor of Germany and King of Bohemia. This holy woman was passionately beloved by her husband, but as he was a bad man, he made her suffer a martyrdom by his insane jealousy. There was at the Court a great Saint called John of Nepomac, who had been chosen confessor to the Court and preacher to the Emperor. This was a difficult post to occupy for a Saint, and John risked his life as often as he preached a sermon. The Empress chose the Saint for her own confessor, and by the help of his advice made rapid strides in the way of sanctity. She had always been devout and kind; now she became doubly pious and charitable, and the very shadow of sin made her shudder. But Wenceslaus could not bear to see his wife so holy, nor did he like to see how much time she spent in holy exercises. He began to suspect all kinds of wicked things of his holy wife, and an intense and wicked desire came over him to know the secrets of her heart. There was only one in the world who could know those secrets, so Wenceslaus made up his mind that that one should tell him all he knew. Jane confessed to John the priest; John should tell him what he heard in Confession. This was the wicked Emperor's resolution.

But Wenceslaus had to do with a priest of God. The order came to the confessor that he was to disclose all he knew of the Empress's conscience. John refused respectfully but firmly. A very short time after his refusal he was put into prison and chained with heavy manacles. As long as he refused to do the Emperor's bidding so long should he remain there, was the decree.

But after a little time a courtier came from the King to say that John was expected at a great banquet to be given in his honour, and that on a certain day he was to present himself at Court. John obeyed; he took his place at table, and was much honoured by the Emperor. After the repast all the guests were dismissed except the Saint. The Emperor retained him for a private, confidential talk. They sat on for some time conversing on indifferent matters, though the Saint well knew what was on the Sovereign's mind. At last the name of the Empress was spoken, and once more the Saint was pressed to tell what he knew of her conscience. John gave the same answer. He knew less of what he knew in Confession than of what he knew nothing at all. Wenceslaus was white with passion; he ordered his guest to be taken straight to the dungeons, and there to be tortured. John was racked, burning torches were applied to his side, and he was roasted over a slow fire. One word only would have sufficed to free him from pain, but by the mercy of God and his own constancy John would not utter that word. The Emperor, instead of being overcome by such heroism, hardened his heart still more. It is not for nothing that he has been called the "Drunkard" and the "Slothful." His passions had corrupted his mind until all humanity had vanished. Seeing that he could not overcome the Saint by torture, he once more released him, and John went about his priestly functions again. But the Saint knew well enough that his trial was not over. He prepared his soul for another combat. And he was wise.

On the eve of Ascension Day some ruffianly men called at John's house in the dead of night, carried out the Saint in their arms, and dropped him into the river that runs between the Great and Little Prague. He was to be drowned in the dark of the night, that no one might know of his execution. But such was not God's will. A cry was heard in the city early on the day of the feast, and thousands flocked to the river to see a great miracle. There, floating upon the quiet waters, with a halo of light around him, with a finger upon his dead lips, was John the martyr-priest, who had loved silence better than riches, and had kept the seal of Confession from a wicked tyrant. See how God strengthens His servants! Do you think we need fear when priests are so strong to suffer and to endure?

A cry was heard in the city

BEDE'S HOME-GOING

St. Bede the Venerable, May 27

Venerable Bede might be called *Father Deo Gratias*, for he lived thanking God and died thanking Him. Children do not like to think of death-beds, but I think the youngest among you would like to have been with the English Saint when he was dying. He was old, and his life had been spent in writing and studying and composing things for the glory of God. When he did not work he prayed. And he prayed so much that people said it was a wonder he had time for anything else. And he wrote so much that people said it was a wonder he could have prayed so much. That makes one understand that prayer does not hinder, but rather helps work. For those have done most who have prayed most.

Bede was Mass priest of Jarrow—that is, he had to say the daily Mass for the monastery. Jarrow was a fine old convent, where Bede had a school of young monks whom he taught, and these scholars of his amounted to six hundred. When Bede was not in school he was writing his learned books, which have come down to us and which are the glory of the Anglo-Saxon Church. But we must skip all the dear Saint's life if we want to read of his death.

He was busy dictating his translation of the Gospel of St. John. He had got to the words in the sixth chapter, "But what are these among so many?" so there were fifteen more chapters of the Gospel to be translated. It was the Tuesday before Ascension Thursday, and Bede was ill. His feet were swollen and his breathing was heavy. But he went through the day dictating as usual. Sometimes he would say quite cheerfully: "Take down what I say quickly, for I know not how long I may last, or whether my Maker may not take me soon."

One night the Saint did not sleep at all. He gave thanks all the night long. On Wednesday he urged his scribes to make haste. The Rogation procession interrupted the morning's work. All the young scholars had to go into the fields and sing their litanies, to ask a blessing upon the fruits of the earth. So long ago, children, the Church was keeping her sacred times, just as she keeps them now. As the day closed in a child-brother said: "Dearest Master, one chapter still is wanting; can you bear our asking about it?" He answered, yes, he could, but they should write quickly. Then, when three o'clock came, the Saint begged all his dear brothers in religion to come around him. He wanted to say goodbye, and to give them presents. He was a poor monk, children, so his presents were poor—a few peppercorns, a few grains of incense, and a few little handkerchiefs. The rest of the day passed in joy until the evening, when the boy again said: "Master, there is yet one sentence not written!" He answered: "Write quickly!" The boy wrote and then said: "Now it is done"; and he held up the page. "Thou saidst the truth, '*consummatum est*'" (it is finished). "Take my head into thy hands, for it is very pleasant to me to sit facing my old praying-place, and thus to call upon my Father." And so they laid him on the floor of his cell, and he sang: "Glory be to the Father and to the Son and to the Holy Ghost!" and just as he said "the Holy Ghost," he gave up his spirit, and went to his heavenly Home.

Is not that a beautiful death? You would not have been afraid to stand there and see that joyous old man go forth with his ascending Master, would you? It was the eve of the Ascension, when the monks were singing the first Vespers of the feast that Bede was taken Home. How well he must have prayed, or he never would have wanted to sit and look at the place of his prayer. St. John Berchmans asked when he was dying to have his crucifix in his hand, and his rosary and his Book of Rules. Because in his life he had loved them and used them well, so in death he loved the sight of them, and the thought of what they had been to him was a comfort.

Will all of you dear little readers say with me every Ascension Day at twelve o'clock—the hour our dear Lord is thought to have gone up to Heaven—ten

"*Glorias*" in honour of our ascending Lord, and in union with St. Bede's last prayer, "Glory be to the Father and to the Son and to the Holy Ghost!" ? Thus we will commend to him our last hours, and beg of him to look after us when we come to die.

A CHRISTIAN CÆSAR

Blessed Cæsar de Bus, May 28

YOUNG Cæsar de Bus was a valiant soldier. He fought against the heretics under Charles IX, and, what is more praiseworthy, kept himself unspotted amidst the licence of war. Peace was proclaimed, and the young noble returned to Paris, and lived the gay life of a civilian in the gay capital. What war could not do, peace in idleness accomplished. Cæsar fell away from virtue, and became an outcast from God.

One day Cæsar, splendidly attired, left his house to seek some evening pleasure. He fell fainting to the ground. His evil living had told upon his health. In the sickness which followed he had time to think, and God came to him with a loving invitation. Cæsar made up his mind he would repent, leave the world, and become a priest. He rose up from his sick-bed a different man. But there were years of struggle before him; the backward path was thorny. It was well for him that he had two devoted friends who had determined together to fight in prayer for his soul, for their prayers prevailed. De Bus on his way to

Avignon met with some companions of his evil days. They, not knowing the change that had come over him, asked him to a ball. There is no harm in going to a ball, but in this case there was danger for the young penitent. He danced gaily till late at night, but left the house feeling sad and discouraged; his conscience was ill at ease, and the things of God seemed dull and impossible. As he wended his way homeward, he passed a convent of Poor Clares. The religious were chanting the morning hours. The sound of sweet voices and the restrained dignity of the chant brought back to the young man's heart all the longing for the good and the best that he had so recently felt, but which seemed to have been put to flight by the wild dancing and music of that hot night. He went home and prayed for strength to break with the world. Another turning-point was vouchsafed to him.

One day Cæsar was in church, dressed in his Court robes, rapier hanging from his jewelled belt and plumed hat by his side. He saw the sacristan coming towards him with a lighted candle. He knew that the summons meant an act of faith, trying to human nature. Cæsar rose instantly, took the candle, and followed the sacristan. He was to accompany the Blessed Sacrament to some poor bedside. So gallant Cæsar braved the scorn of his friends, and in his Court attire took part in the lowly procession. This last test, faithfully stood, brought the young man fresh grace. From that moment he never looked back. He broke with the world, studied for the priesthood, and became the founder of a pious association of priests for the teaching of Catechism to the young and ignorant.

Cæsar had been a soldier of the King. After his conversion he was still a soldier, and that of the great King. He had still to fight hard in his own heart. For twenty-five years he was tempted with evil desires. But he bore all his sufferings to make reparation for his past life; and when the thought of his sins overwhelmed him, he would say: "I have sinned indeed, but I have borne the cross." Saddest of all, there came upon the holy man a total blindness that prevented him from saying Mass. To one like him, who knew so well the value of a Mass, this was a grievous affliction. But Our Lord can give with one hand what He takes away with another, and we may be sure Cæsar was not left without every means necessary to overcome.

Now if you think of this life, you will see what I see: how easy it is to keep God's grace—how much harder it is to get it back. And that is only just. If we throw away money or presents given us by our parents or friends, they are not so ready to give us more. If we take care of them, and use them wisely, they give more freely. You are young now, and it is well for you to take counsel with yourselves, and see how you mean to walk as you grow up. Keep your virtue by the grace of God. Don't count on winning a portion back, and making up for what you have lost. Though, should you lose your virtue, then hope with humble, loving hearts, and do

your best, God helping, to recover it again. May 28 is
the Venerable Cæsar's feast. Remember to say a prayer
to him to help you to keep what he so courageously
won back.

JUNE

ST. ROBERT

St. Robert of Newminster, June 7

A LITTLE Robert, who is perhaps not quite a Saint, asked me some time ago to write about his patron. Now, there is more than one St. Robert, but as we are mostly English, St. Robert of Newminster will interest us most, I think.

St. Robert of Newminster lived about the year 1100, when Henry I was crowned; he lived through Stephen's unhappy reign, and died when Henry II, firm of hand and skilled in ruling, had been five years upon the throne.

Most likely the boy Robert in his Yorkshire home felt little of political disturbance, for he did not mix with the world at all. He shrank even from the company of his fellows, and would rather have read and prayed than have played and amused himself. Perhaps this sounds strange to you, but it is not as strange as it seems. It is only when people have tried how delightful prayer is that they can understand how the Saints could pray so much. It is like two persons eating. One is well and enjoys his food; he can take a good quantity and relish all he takes; he looks forward to his meals, and takes an interest in them. The other is ill; dislikes the taste, smell, sight of things to eat; can only take a small quantity, and feels no better for it—worse perhaps.

Imperfect, tepid people are more or less like this invalid. They don't relish prayer; they get bored, are not interested; they only do what is absolutely necessary, and not even that if they can help it. The Saints are like the sound person, eager for the time of prayer, making as much of it as possible, turning it to good account, and most happy only when they are at prayer. So we won't think of the Saints as a queer set, will we? but just remember that the difference between them and us is as between a sound person and an invalid; they are the sound, we are the invalids, and it is our business to get sound as soon as possible.

When Robert had been some years a priest at York, he entered the Benedictine monastery of Our Lady in York, but he left it with twelve others to live a still harder life. They all settled on the River Skeld, near Ripon, and built themselves huts made of hurdles, covered with turf for roofs. You might suppose it would be great fun to live in airy cabins like that, but I believe it sounds funnier than it actually is. That sort of dwelling is apt to be extremely cold and draughty and insecure. And after all, one does like to feel sure that one's roof will not fall off or the walls fall in, which these monks could certainly not feel. Then they were often very hungry, and had hardly enough clothes to wear. You see, it takes a good deal of material to clothe thirteen monks, and a good deal of food to feed them. For though they fasted often, they had to eat sometimes. The people round about were poor, too, so that they couldn't help much.

But God was looking after His monks. When two trying years had gone by, He sent them a rich novice called Hugh, who brought all his money with him, and then the monks began to build the splendid abbey called "Fountains" Abbey, near Ripon. It was called "Fountains" because of the clear springs in the grounds. It is an exquisite spot, with running water, rich vegetation, and stately beeches. Only the ruins of the monastery are to be seen now, but the loveliness of the place can still be admired much as it was in the time of the holy monks.

There St. Robert lived for many years among his brethren. Never was a murmur heard, never was a look of sadness seen. They laboured hard, they slept little, but they were happy and joyous. And St. Robert was the happiest of all, because he was the most holy.

One Easter Sunday St. Robert came to the refectory, but he could hardly eat anything. The brethren pressed him, but he had fasted so long that he could bear nothing solid. After a great deal of persuasion the monks made him take a little bread and honey. It was out of the common, and the Saint was reluctant. It was brought to him on a plate. He looked at it, smiled, shook his head, and bade a Brother carry it to the gate and give it to the poor. A young man with a shining face took the gift and disappeared. At the next meal there descended from Heaven the very plate that had been given to the poor. It was empty, to show that the gift had been received in Heaven.

A great Baron visited Fountains Abbey one day, and was so edified with the monks that he built them a new monastery, and called it Newminster. St. Robert became Abbot there, and it was thus he got his name. When he died his soul was seen going up to Heaven, and a voice was heard to say: "Enter now, my friend!"

I hope my little Robert admires his patron Saint, and that, like him, he will be good to the poor.

STORIES ABOUT ST. ANTHONY

St. Anthony of Padua, June 13

O NE DAY a Jew came to St. Anthony to discuss with him about the real presence of Our Lord upon the altar. Guillard, the Jew, had been the most wicked of a faction that had persecuted the Christians, and he had opposed the Word of God in every way in his power. After much prayer and discussion St. Anthony asked the man why he could not believe in the statement of the Son of God, that really in the Blessed Sacrament there is the Body and Blood of Christ. The Jew replied that it was impossible, and unless he saw a wonderful miracle, he could never believe. "Brother Anthony," he said, "I will renounce the faith of my fathers if your God will do for you the following miracle. I will starve my mule for three days. At the end of that time I will come with it into the public square, and offer it a feed of oats. You, on the other hand, shall come in with the Sacred Host in your hands. If my mule refuses its meal and prostrates itself before the monstrance, I will become a Catholic."

Inspired by the Holy Ghost, Anthony accepted the challenge. For three days the Apostle fasted and prayed, and obtained prayers from all whom he knew. When the day came, Guillard, the Jew, entered the market-place with a rejoicing crowd of adherents. Anthony also approached, carrying in his hands the Sacred Host in the monstrance, and followed by crowds singing canticles of praise. The Saint stopped in front of the mule, and, hushing the crowd, spoke to the poor hungry beast, adjuring it in the Name of its Creator to come and adore the God Who created it. At the same moment one of the Jews offered the mule a feed of oats. The mule, without a moment's hesitation, brushed past the tempting meal, went up to where the Saint stood, and worshipped on its knees. A deafening shout rent the air; many of the Jews were converted— among them the owner of the mule, who had given the terrible challenge.

Another day a large crowd had collected to hear the Saint preach. They were out in a field because there was no room in any of the churches. Heavy clouds hung overhead, and every moment a deluge of rain was expected. The audience looked frightened, and made ready to leave the field. St. Anthony promised those who remained that they should not be wet. The rain came down in streams, and soaked through the impatient people who went home, but spared those who stayed to listen.

But the most touching story of all is that of the little Holy Child's visit to St. Anthony, a picture of which artists have loved to paint.

One day Anthony was in the palace of a great and good man called Chateauneuf. The Saint was alone in his room, when it was filled with light of so dazzling a kind that mortal eye could hardly bear the brilliance. In the light there shone forth Our Lord in the figure of a little Child of superhuman beauty. He nestled in the Saint's arms, and caressed him, just as a loving babe might do, filling Anthony's soul with a bliss that we shall not know until we reach our heavenly Home. The lord of the palace came back, and noticed the brilliant light coming out of the Saint's room. He entered, and asked the Saint what was taking place. The Saint had a joyful message to give his benefactor, for his heavenly Visitor had inspired him with a knowledge of the future. "He revealed to me," said Anthony, "that your house would be prosperous beyond all hope as long as it remains faithful to Catholicity; but it will be overwhelmed with misfortunes if ever it forsakes the Faith." The prophecy was fulfilled to the letter.

And now I am going to finish with the pretty little verse to St. Anthony that you will find in your "Alphabet of the Saints" if you are so lucky as to possess one. The book is only a shilling, and you would love to read what is said about the Saints all in rhyme.

SAINT ANTONY *of* PADUA, *Confessor. Friar Minor of the Order of Saint Francis of Assisi. Born in Portugal, 1196. Died at Padua, 1231. Feast, June 13.*

St ANTONY *of* PADUA

A is ANTONY of PADUA, a Friar wise and kind;
He never had a penny, but he never seemed to mind;
He was very fond of reading, but the book he read the most
Was the book that tells of GOD, the Father, Son and Holy Ghost;
He was very fond of children, but the Child he loved the best
Was the little Infant JESUS, as He lay on Mary's breast;
And once when he was reading with the Gospel on a stand
Little JESUS stood upon it and caressed him with His hand.
Now that ANTONY'S in Heaven, if you ever lose your toys,
I advise you to invoke him, for he's good to girls and boys.

THE FISHES THAT HEARD A SERMON

More Stories of St. Anthony

ONE DAY Anthony was sent to Rimini in Italy to preach to the heretics of that city. Rimini is on the sea-coast not far from Urbino. Anthony preached his most lovely sermons; he spoke, with his eyes full of tears, of Our Blessed Lord and His love for man. But few came to listen, and of those few some mocked. So, very sad at heart, Anthony turned to the seashore, and sat upon a low rock just where the river ran into the sea. Then a thought came to him: he would preach to God's creatures, the fishes of the sea, and he would see if they would listen to his words. So he stood upon this rock, and stretched out his hand as if he were speaking to men.

"Hear the Word of God, O ye fishes of the sea, since the infidel heretics refuse to hear it!" No sooner had he said the words than there was a splashing and a surging of the waters; a great multitude of fish of all sizes and kinds arranged themselves before the Saint. Some clustered close up to the bank—these were the smallest fish; next to them, further from the shallow water, was the next size fish, and so on, till there came right at the back the largest fish of all. Never before had there been seen such a multitude in those waters. And they all listened with their heads out of the water and their eyes turned to the preacher. Sometimes they bowed their heads quite low, sometimes they opened their mouths as if they were drinking in his words with great reverence. When St. Anthony saw all these eager faces looking out of the water at him, and all of them so gentle and quiet, he began his sermon. He told them how much they had to thank God for; they had a beautiful element to live in, they had sweet water and salt just as they liked; they were fed and protected and blessed. At the deluge they alone of all the animals had survived: one of their number had saved the Prophet Jonas; one had brought in its mouth the tribute money for Our Lord and His Vicar, St. Peter. Their great Creator had eaten fish before and after His Resurrection, which was a wonderful privilege for their kind. Then as Anthony saw more and more fish coming to join the multitude he raised his voice and cried out: "Blessed be God Eternal, because the fishes of the water give Him more reverence than do the heretics; and the animals that have no reason pay more heed unto His Word than unbelieving men."

As St. Anthony was preaching to the fishes the rumour of the miracle reached the town; people flocked to the seashore to see the fishes; they came near

and marvelled at the upturned faces of the senseless
animals. They were stricken with shame by the grace
of God, and stayed to listen with humility, where they
had only thought to mock. Then St. Anthony spoke to
them of God's mercy and His love, of the doctrines of
the Catholic Church, of pardon and penance. Still the
fishes remained listening and quiet. Nor did they move
until St. Anthony had finished his sermon. Then he
raised his hands and gave them a big blessing, and told
them they might go and praise God. After that sermon
to the fishes St. Anthony stayed long in Rimini, but
never again was there wanting to him a good, sensible
audience.

SCOUTS

I AM very much hoping that you children have read, or, better still, are reading "Scouting for Boys." It is not spiritual reading, nor is the writer a Catholic, but there is much in the book that is good for everyone to know and *to do*—especially to do. A boy who models himself upon Major-General Baden-Powell's idea of a manly scout, and practises his religion in the same whole-hearted manner, would reach a very high perfection. The book teaches you how to hold yourself, how to walk, to work, to sleep, to observe, to play, to read, and hundreds of other things; how to behave towards the lowest and highest, how to be of use in all kinds of emergencies. Better still! Listen to this: "Touch your head with both your hands, and look up into the sky, leaning back as far as you can…while looking up this way, say to God, 'I am yours from top to toe.'" When you breathe you are told to thank God for His pure, fresh air. When you see others off at the station you are recommended to pray for them, that God may take care of them on their journey, and not of them only, but of all those in the train with them. Such thoughts sanctify life and consecrate body and soul to God.

At first one might think that St. Aloysius Gonzaga could not have any likeness to a *scout*. But when you look closer it does not seem impossible at all. For a scout has to be kind to all: he has to be good to those younger than himself and to the old; he has to be unselfish, and willing to take up the hardest work; he has to be religious, and keep himself well in hand. Now, St. Aloysius did all this, and a very great deal more, of course. For he was a perfect soldier of Christ, whereas a scout is only just ordinary. Let us see.

When Aloysius was four years old, his father, who was a Marquis and a General, took him with him to the camp in Casal, which he was going to hold against the enemy. His little son and heir had a full suit of armour made for him—helmet, with nodding plume, cuirass, sword and belt, and powder-flask, in which there was actually some powder, and an arquebus—that is, a kind of gun. But the child made the arquebus explode one day, so he was deprived of his powder, much to the relief of his fellow-soldiers, I should think. But the smell and the excitement of the explosion roused the soldier in the baby. When the garrison was asleep, Aloysius stole out to the court where he knew the soldiers kept their arms, and he appropriated some powder from a flask. With this he hastened to a small field-piece which stood upon the ramparts. He loaded the

gun, and stood joyously by as the explosion sounded
loud and menacing all over the castle. The Marquis
was roused from his siesta, and immediately donned
his Judge's robes. This was a mutiny, he thought, or
a signal for an insurrection. He sat in state to receive
the evildoer. Who should be brought in but his tiny
son! The boy explained exactly what had happened.
The father pretended to be angry, and was imposing a
suitable punishment, when all the soldiers, who loved
Aloysius, begged for mercy and a free pardon. There
was the making of a soldier in that little child—only
Our Lord wanted him to be a different type of hero.

From his birth to the time he became a Jesuit, the
boy was surrounded with servants. They ministered to
him everywhere, so Aloysius had many opportunities
of being a good scout. He spoke to them all as if they
were brothers. He did not like to command them;
he asked them very seldom for anything, and then he
spoke as if to an equal. When he became a religious
he tried to do all the hardest and most disagreeable
work. He helped in the kitchen, washed plates and
dishes, collected the scraps for the poor. He swept
the rooms, and went about removing cobwebs most
carefully. For a long time he had charge of the lamps
in the passages and rooms; he had to clean them, and
fill them with oil. I don't know whether any of you
know what sort of work that is, but I can assure you
that in those days, when there was nothing but oil,
and that not of the finest kind, the business of the

lamps was no small one. Very like a true scout all this, isn't it?

Not long before Aloysius died, there broke out in Rome a terrible pestilence, and the Saint got leave to nurse the sick in the hospital. We go to the hospitals sometimes, but what we see in those beautifully organized places would give us no idea of what a plague hospital in Rome at that time was. Here the *late Marquis* tended the sick and dying with superhuman love and tenderness. The servers' work was to wash and wait upon the sick; they had to cleanse their wounds, and do the most revolting services for them. All this did Aloysius, taking upon himself those patients who were the least attractive. Like a scout, isn't it?

That was the last great work Aloysius did upon earth. The terrible time in the hospital undermined his health; he caught the disease, and died a few weeks later. Now, I have not told you how great the dear young Saint was at praying; how he wore his knees to the bone kneeling; how he kept recollection by training his senses till they obeyed the lightest wish of his heavenly soul; how he longed to die and go to God. All this you must read about yourselves, and see whether Saints are not the right kind of scouts and heroes.

SS. PETER AND PAUL

June 29

THERE ARE some very ugly words in our English language—not ugly in themselves, but according to the way they are used. There is nothing disagreeable about the word "soft," but when one is called "soft" one does not particularly like it. That is because the word is misapplied. A soft cushion is all very well; a soft bed comfortable and reasonable enough. But a soft boy or a soft girl—well, it does not sound a right or reasonable thing. Why? Because we were never meant to be soft. We were meant to be robust, hard with ourselves, strong of will, able to endure and overcome.

Far, far away in the West, in a place called Manitoba, a long time ago, there were Indians who did not want their children to become like European children. Do you know why? The reason is not flattering, but it is wholesome to see ourselves as others see us sometimes. This is what the Indians said: "We are not like you; you were made of white earth, we were made of black. We are real men; you are children. You need so many things that we can do without—lots of things for eating, for clothing, for sleeping and playing with. We do not want our children to become like that."

I think the Indians are right. It is babyish to want so much, to be always wanting more and more meals, more and more drinks; ices when the weather is hot, and fruit at all times. It is babyish to be always thinking of such trifles as clothes, and sweets, and toys, or of medicine and cures, when we ought to have other and much better things to think of. We have got to work, to suffer, and to do good. It is no use shirking things. Toothache will come even if my father is a dentist, and measles won't keep away even if my mother is a trained nurse. I must feel cold even if I am a princess, which I am not. And I shall feel tired, I hope, sometimes, even if I am the lord of a manor.

Now, I have for my title the word "heroes." And I seem to be thinking of anything but such splendid people. And yet it was the thought of my heroes that made me begin like this. St. Peter is one of them. St. Paul is another. They were great heroes because they were Saints. You cannot possibly be a Saint without being a hero. So that is how I know that these two Apostles were heroes. Now, St. Peter certainly did not always act like a hero, because he was not always one. He was afraid oftener than he ought to have been; he would have got out of all suffering if he could. He couldn't bear to be sneered at; he was ashamed of Our Lord, and denied Him. That does not look much like a hero, does it? But then he conquered all this cowardice; he overcame his fear; he braved the sneers of great people; he learnt to love pain and insult. Once he was scourged in the Sanhedrin before all the nobles of Israel; his back was bared, and the lash came down upon his flesh. But Peter and his best friend, John, went away from the Council rejoicing. They had learned that suffering for Our Lord's Name is really sweet. And when you have learnt that much, and have put it into practice, you are very little short of a hero, if at all.

St. Paul once hated the name of Christ; he persecuted all who professed themselves Christians. He sought them out in their houses; he hunted them down as if they had been animals. But God called, and Paul answered. He was struck from his horse as he was riding hard to Damascus. He fell a Jew; he rose up a Christian. "Who art Thou, Lord?" he asked the invisible force that had struck him. "Jesus of Nazareth, Whom thou persecutest," was the answer.

After that there came loving years of hard service. As he had persecuted, so did he serve; as he had hated, so did he love.

Is it not better to live lives like these than soft, namby-pamby lives that the very savages sneer at and think unworthy? I wouldn't like to be below a heathen, whatever happened; and I am sure you would not.

JULY

ST. PHOCAS

July 3

Outside the city of Sinope there lived a wealthy gardener. He spent all his time tilling, sowing, and planting. When the day's work was done, he would seek out a quiet spot and pray the greater part of the night. He gave his money to the poor, and lived the life of a hermit and a Saint.

One day he heard the tramping of feet some distance from his house. He listened; the steps came nearer. They had the distinct sound of drilled men. As they approached, Phocas was able to see soldiers in the Roman garb, probably in quest of some criminal. He went out to meet them, and graciously offered them hospitality for the night. The soldiers were taken with his manner, and told him their errand. They were in search of a Christian whose name was Phocas. They had orders to hunt him down and kill him without waiting for a trial, so odious to the Emperor was the crime he was guilty of. Phocas listened and smiled, but said nothing. With his own hands he prepared a hearty meal, waited upon his guests, and entertained them with cheerful discourse. When they were in bed he went into his garden and dug his own grave, then spent the rest of the night in prayer. In the morning he called his guests and gave them breakfast. When they had finished their meal he told them that he himself was Phocas of whom they were in search, and bid them do the Emperor's bidding. The soldiers were struck with sorrow; how could they put to death one who had done them nothing but good? But Phocas showed them that death was for him a gain, that he longed to go to his Lord. Then they struck off his head, and a moment's pain brought the generous martyr to his Master's feet.

The sailors of the Black Sea sing hymns to the honour of St. Phocas, and a portion of gain that falls to their lot is set aside for the poor, called "Phocas's part." Does not virtue last a long time? Phocas lived about the year 300; he was only a gardener, and yet for all time he is being venerated for his noble generosity and love of Our Lord.

ST. ELIZABETH OF PORTUGAL

July 8

ST. ELIZABETH, Queen of Hungary, had a niece called after her, Elizabeth, who likewise became a Saint and was canonized. This child was the daughter of Peter III of Aragon. Her mother was a Sicilian Princess, and she married a King. From her childhood Elizabeth was a tender, gentle girl, and all through her life had to play the peacemaker in her family. There was at one time war to the knife between her husband and her son; Elizabeth interceded, and separated the combatants. There was a feud between the King of Castile and his cousin; another between her own brother and Ferdinand IV. Each dispute was settled amicably by the prayers and tears of the Saint. So you see she had not a very happy time in her royal home!

When the Saint was twelve years old she was married to Dionysius, King of Portugal. He loved her because she was beautiful, rich, royal, and witty; but he was a wicked man, and followed his passions wherever they led him. He allowed her to serve God after her own fashion, and secretly admired her for her goodness and piety. At the same time he watched her carefully and jealously, for, being evil himself, he imagined horrible things to be possible to her. But neither suspicion, nor cruelty, nor insult, troubled Elizabeth. She bore her suffering with the greatest calm; she sought to please her ungrateful husband with unwearying patience, and never let her prayers nor good deeds stand in the way of her duty to the King. But Dionysius was long incredulous. He could not believe that anyone so wronged as his holy Queen could be so forgiving and true.

One day a wicked young page came to the King, and dropped some words as to Elizabeth's conduct. She favoured a young page too much, he said; the boy was winning her affections. It was the duty of the King to look to it. Instead of horsewhipping the malicious boy, Dionysius listened and believed, and conceived a diabolic hatred for the Queen's innocent young page. One morning he visited a lime-kiln and ordered the lime-burner to throw into the furnace the youth who should come to him with the question, "Have you fulfilled the King's command?" for that messenger would well deserve the awful death, he said. Shortly after, the King despatched the Queen's page to ask the fatal question, and awaited with gnawing impatience the result. Two hours passed, and no message had come from the kiln. Dionysius could bear the suspense no longer. He called the calumniator, and bid him go to the lime-burner, and ask whether he had done the King's command. The page did his bidding in breathless haste. No sooner did the lime-burner catch sight of him, and hear his message, than he seized and threw him into the heart of the furnace.

Not long after, the Queen's page came to the King with a bright face and sparkling eyes. The lime-burner had done the King's command, he said. The King grew pale with fear. Was this an apparition! a soul come back from the grave! He questioned the boy. Where had he been? How came he back from the furnace? The page told how he had first gone to hear Mass in the church, how he had waited for a second and a third Mass, according to his custom, but how when these were over he had hastened to do the King's command. When he asked his question of the burner, he had pointed to the furnace, and had grinned unpleasantly, the boy said. Then Dionysius knew that a greater than he had judged the case, and had pronounced guilty and punished the true offender. He was sorry for his sin, and ever after showed his love and veneration for his saintly wife. It was she who nursed him in his last sickness, and prepared him for death with more than a mother's patience, and she had the happiness of seeing him reconciled to God.

Elizabeth died at the age of sixty-five. She received the Holy Viaticum on her knees, and shortly after the Extreme Unction; after that she sank gradually. Her favourite prayer was: "Mary, Mother of grace, Mother of mercy, defend us from the wicked enemy, and receive us at the hour of our death."

THE PERSIANS AND THE GNATS

St. James of Nisibis, July 15

THERE ARE wonderful stories told of St. James, Bishop of Nisibis. But first of all I must tell you who he was. Nisibis is in Mesopotamia, and James was born there about the year 350. For a long time he lived like a hermit, all alone on the top of a mountain, eating only raw wild roots and herbs. He was dressed in a tunic and cloak made of coarse goat's hair. People are very quick as a rule in finding out a Saint, and it was not long before a number climbed the rocks that led to James's cell. But James was not a selfish solitary, if there are any. He found time to go down into towns and villages to strengthen people's faith and instruct young converts; he worked many miracles, and often prophesied about things to come, so that men and women heard him gladly, and believed his word. The tyrant, Maximin II, was reigning, and James suffered torments for his Faith.

One day he was made a Bishop, but still he went on living his austere life, eating his coarse vegetables and living in the open. Once a troop of beggars saw the Bishop coming down a road; they made up a plot between them, that one of them should pretend to be dead, and that the others should beg the Saint to give them something to bury him with. "When James came up with the beggars, they asked him for money, for their companion lay there dead, they said. The Saint prayed over the supposed corpse, and asked God to forgive him his sins. Then he gave the men a sum of money sufficient for their pretended purpose, and passed on his way. But when the men came to rouse their comrade and share with him the booty, they found that he was really dead. In terror they called the Saint back, and implored him to pray for the man, explaining to him with great sorrow the wicked trick they had played.

James prayed earnestly, and then took the beggar by the hand; he stood up alive and well.

Sapor II, the great Persian King, besieged Nisibis with a splendid army. There were soldiers on foot, and there were riders on horses and elephants; there were warlike engines for scaling walls and beating down fortresses. But after trying for sixty-three days he was compelled to raise the siege and retire, for Bishop James and his flock prayed to God with all their souls, night and day. Some time later, however, another Persian army under another leader, called Chosroës, came and sat down before Nisibis. Chosroës was a great warrior, and he and his soldiers had come victors in the fight. He cut off all the avenues of approach to the town, and tried to make a breach in the walls with his battering-rams and by undermining. But all his efforts were fruitless. Then he threw up a dam to stop the River Mygdon, and when the water was piled up high as a wall, he demolished the dam and let the water burst into the city. The Persians who were looking on shouted with wild joy; their labour was ended, they thought, the city must fall. But as they followed the rushing water into the town they found to their dismay and surprise that the inhabitants had built another wall between them and the new peril, and so stout and strong was it that it stood firm against the foaming tide. St. James had watched and prayed and instructed the garrison, and they had followed his advice like docile children and had proved successful. But the enemy was still without, so the soldiers begged the holy Bishop to go up and pray for the destruction of the Persian hordes. The meek old man could not pray for the destruction of anyone, so he asked God to have pity on his people, and save them from the horrors of a long siege. "Lord, Thou art able by the weakest means to humble the pride of Thy enemies; defeat these multitudes by an army of gnats." This was the Saint's prayer. Scarcely were the words spoken than clouds of gnats and flies came pouring in upon the Persian host. They got into the ears and nostrils of the horses, into the trunks of the elephants, and so enraged the animals that they threw their riders, and made a fearful havoc in the camp. A famine and pestilence followed, and the King left Nisibis with the loss of 20,000 men.

When St. James died he was buried in the city he had loved so much, but later his relics were carried to Constantinople. The Saint was a writer too. I will only quote what he says of Holy Communion, because the words will show you that holy and learned men in the fourth century believed exactly as we do about the Blessed Sacrament of the altar. He says: "None will be cleansed unless they be washed in the laver of Baptism, and have received the Body and Blood of Christ. For blood is expiated by this Blood, and the body cleansed by this Body. Be assiduous in prayer, and above all prayer place that which Our Lord has taught us. When you pray remember your friends and me a sinner."

"I'LL PAY HIM OUT!"

St. John Gualbert, July 12

DID you ever think that? Did your blood ever boil to give back with interest the injury you had received? A tight sort of feeling comes over the heart; the tips of one's hands itch to strike, or the tip of the tongue tingles with eagerness to say unkind things. What do you do when you feel like this? I know what the tempter says to one: "Oh, give it to him jolly hard; then you will feel all right again." The tempter is the father of lies, so of course we cannot expect the truth from him. "Forgive and forget," says the Angel of light, and he cannot lie, so it would be well to follow his advice. Now for my story.

A young nobleman named John Gualbert lived in Florence about 1173. He had an only brother whom he loved passionately. The two had been brought up with great care, and taught to love God. John as he grew up forgot many of the holy things he had learned at Catechism, and followed his own inclinations. He loved pleasure too much; he was proud of his high birth, and he did not attend particularly well to his religious duties. Now, this is a dangerous way of living, for there is sure to come a time when a big temptation arises in the mind. And then a sacrifice has to be made, or sin will be committed. The temptation came to John with an awful trouble. News was brought to him one day that his only brother was murdered. White with passion, John declared that he would never rest until he had the murderer's life. It is horrible to think that the father urged his son to take revenge. And revenge became the absorbing thought of John's life. Wherever he went he hoped to meet his enemy, and do to him as he had done.

One Good Friday John was riding with his servant home to Florence. They came to a narrow pass and John saw another horseman advance. He recognized him at once; it was his brother's murderer. John drew his sword, and rushed upon his enemy. But the other, alighting from his horse, threw himself upon his knees and begged for mercy, begged it for the sake of the Redeemer Who had died that day for their sake. John's heart was softened. Christ stretched upon the Cross had prayed for His murderers. Who was he to withhold pardon from one who asked in His name? He raised the unfortunate man from the ground, and said: "I can refuse nothing that is asked of me in the name of Jesus Christ. I not only give you your life, but also my friendship for ever. Pray that God may forgive me my sin."

They parted. John went straight to the church hard by, and knelt at the foot of the crucifix. There he poured out his heart in prayer, praying God to forgive him his sins. Then a miracle happened. The figure of Our Lord moved; the arms were loosened; they stretched out and took the kneeling penitent into their embrace.

From that day John walked quickly on the road to sanctity. He founded an Order, and established many monasteries, and God showered blessings upon him. And the beginning of all this good was that forgiveness, which had cost him so much. Shall we go and do likewise?

Blessed are the Merciful~

BROTHER GILES

Blessed Giles of Assisi

WHEN Henry III was reigning in England, there lived in Italy a lay brother of the Order of St. Francis. He was a very simple monk, and if anybody had been asked what they thought of him, I suspect they would have said that he was very good, but perhaps *not quite all there*. I mean some would have said that—not the best kind of people, but those who judge by appearances, and care for the things of this world. Now, it was just because he cared nothing for the things of this world that Giles the lay brother was rather looked down upon by worldlings. The only thing the matter with him was that he had given his whole big heart to God, and when you do that other things do not count much.

One day Giles went out; he wanted to find a master who would teach him how to serve God, and give up all things. On his journey he came across Francis of Assisi; they fell into conversation, and Giles knew he had found the man he wanted. As they came back a poor woman asked an alms. Francis had nothing with him, so he told his new companion to give her his cloak. Without a moment's hesitation Giles gave his cloak, and was filled with joy at the thought of renouncing everything for the love of God at the word of obedience. Now, you see, that is just the sort of thing some people would call *mad*—not only to give away necessary things, but to rejoice in the giving. But Giles did other things quite as insane according to the world.

St. Louis of France was King. He heard of good Brother Giles, and he made up his mind he would go and see him. So he journeyed to Perugia in a pilgrim's robe, and asked at the convent for the lay brother Giles. Nobody knew the King, but no sooner had Giles cast his eyes upon him than he knew him. Without a word he took the holy King in his arms; then the two—King and peasant—knelt and prayed side by side. After a fervent prayer they rose from their knees and parted without a word! Was that businesslike, do you think? Fancy the things Giles could have asked for! There was nothing Louis would have denied him. How interesting, too, to speak to a great King who had been to the Crusade, who had seen all the heroes of the day, and who was perhaps the greatest hero of all. And Giles misses the opportunity, and only says his prayers, which he could have said at any time just as well.

When it became known in the monastery that the great King of France had visited Brother Giles, there was no end of talk. Why had he not told anyone? Why had he let the monarch go without a word of welcome

from anyone? Brother Giles only smiled. He and St.
Louis understood each other perfectly; there was no
need of talk. He had come for a purpose, and he had
gone when that purpose was accomplished.

None of you will suppose that Brother Giles
became a Saint without any trouble. That no one
does; and a very good thing too. The devil tormented
the simple Brother very much. He tempted him to
sin; he troubled him in a hundred different ways; but
Brother Giles was a match for the fiend. He said the
devil is like a cur who barks ferociously, but will flee
if we kick him well. So he treated him like a cur, and
kicked him well.

Brother Giles had a weakness. He could not hear
holy things mentioned without being taken out of
himself with joy. The thought of God and the Saints,
of Heaven and glory, sent him into a rapture no matter
where he happened to be. Now, the mischievous boys
in the neighbourhood knew this, and they would watch
for him coming down the street, and then cry out:
"Paradise, Paradise!" At once Giles lost all knowledge
of things going on around him, and went into an ecstasy.
Then the boys looked upon his beautiful face, and learnt
what it was to love God above all things. Here again,
you see, worldly people would have thought Giles very
foolish not to have more self-control than to become
rapt in a crowded street, losing time, and making a
spectacle of himself! But then, they are worldly and
don't understand really important things. Blessed Giles

died in 1260, twelve years before Henry III of England.
Would you like to love God like that, or does it seem to
you exaggerated? I hope not.

ST. CHRISTOPHER

I AM going to tell you about St. Christopher, because I have just seen a picture that has set me thinking. The picture shows him to be a man of enormous size; stout of limb, broad of shoulder, thick set, and with well-knit muscles. And such a man was St. Christopher said to be. When he was young he had tried the service of the world, and it had not suited him. So he went to a holy old hermit, and told him that he wanted to serve God, and to serve Him only. At the same time he warned the hermit that it was no good telling him to pray all day long, or to study, or to teach. He could do none of these things. What he wanted was some occupation in which he might use his strength for the service of God. The hermit advised him to take up his abode near a river which in stormy weather was often so swollen as to be quite impassable. Many who tried to get across were drowned, and much misery was caused. Christopher was pleased with the task given him to do. He went to the bank of the river, and built himself a little hut, where he might pray and sleep, and be sheltered from the keen blasts of winter.

For many years the strong man kept the ford, and many a passer-by had he rescued, and many a deed of charity had he done. Once when he was getting old and his strength was not quite what it used to be, he heard a little cry in the night. He raised himself in bed, and listened. Was it the storm, or was it a wail? Surely that was a human cry. In an instant Christopher had girded his robe about him and was on his doorstep. A fierce storm was raging; the water of the river was lashed by the wind, and the current was sweeping all before it. On the opposite bank Christopher saw a tiny child standing; its arms were outstretched, and in a feeble voice it was begging the strong man to carry it over. Christopher took his thick staff in his hand and plunged into the stream. When he gained the opposite bank, he stooped down and took the babe in his arms. It was a tiny child, beautiful and winning in manner. Down the steep bank went Christopher into the flood, planting his staff in the deep mud, and striding through the waves. But how heavy the child was growing! How the little limbs seemed to press upon the stalwart shoulders! Every minute the weight increased; valiantly the man struggled, and onward he waded. Now the perspiration stood upon his forehead; now his limbs ached, and his back was doubled under the burden of the baby-frame. The cold was numbing the sense of feeling, and Christopher thought every moment he would have to give in, and let the current carry him and his sweet charge down the stream. But with an inward prayer he stepped yet more bravely out, and at last, stiff and exhausted, he reached the opposite shore. As he gained dry land, he placed the baby gently down. "Little one," he said, "I have carried many a burden, but none in all the world so heavy as thou art." The child looked up with a sweet smile, and said: "No, Christopher, that may well be. For never before didst thou carry the world's Creator." And with that He vanished, leaving such joy in the heart of the old man as fully made up to him for all his toil.

This is a very pretty legend; but only a legend, I think, or rather an allegory. The stream is the life of man upon earth; the strong man, Christopher, is the Saint making his way through it in spite of temptations and troubles. By his charity to his brethren he attracts his Saviour, and in bearing them he one day finds he is bearing Christ. Or, as the Latin hymn says, he loved Christ so well and bore Him so devoutly in his heart that he is depicted as carrying Him also upon his shoulder. You know that the word *Christopher* means *bearer of Christ*.

Let us be Christophers—ones who love Christ Our Lord, and who for His sake willingly carry our own sorrows and burdens, and also help others to bear theirs.

ⱯUGUST

ST. OSWALD

August 5

WHEN you get big you must read the "Chronicles of St. Bede"; modern people do not write of what they see and hear as did the ancient chroniclers. At least, I don't think so. Most people who write shut their eyes and remember; the chroniclers opened theirs and described. It is the Feast of St. Oswald on Tuesday, August 5. So I read in Bede's "Ecclesiastical History" all that is said of him there.

Oswald was the son of King Ethelfrid. He and his two elder brothers had to flee from the kingdom, and seek refuge with the Scots. They were brought up at Iona, that island of Saints, and were made good Christians. Aidan was their father in Christ. But Eanfrid and Osric, when they came into their kingdom, basely forsook the true God and returned to idolatrous worship. When they were slain by Caedwalla, "the unrighteous instrument of righteous wrath," Oswald, "a man beloved of God," came with a strong hand; he professed the true Faith, and managed in the nine years of his life to strengthen his kingdom, unite Deira and Bernicia, and establish churches all over both countries. Knowing how holy were the monks of Iona, with whom he had been brought up, the King sent to that monastery, and begged the prior to give him a monk to preach the truth and convert the Saxons of his kingdom.

First there came a holy man who was not at all successful, and who, being discouraged, went back to his beloved solitude. On his return a council was held, and the missioner gave his experiences of the people, and of his methods in converting them, and of his ill-success. After his declaration there fell a silence. At last Aidan, the wise, stood up and said he thought the missioner's methods had been too severe. "Methinks, brother, that you were more severe to your unlearned hearers than you ought to have been, and did not at first, according to Apostolic rule, give them the milk of more easy doctrine, till by degrees, being nourished with the Word of God, they should be capable of receiving that which is more perfect, and of performing the higher precepts of God." The assembled brethren heard and agreed with the speaker, and, moreover, determined to send Aidan himself on the Saxon mission. Thus it was that St. Oswald and Aidan worked together for the glory of God. Oswald accompanied the monk wherever he went, and interpreted the Word of God to his ealdormen and thegns, so that many among them were converted. Churches were built in divers places, and the people joyfully flocked together to hear the Word, and gave land and other property to the Church. Oswald bestowed on Aidan the Island of Lindisfarne, because the monk longed for a place to remind him of his own home in Iona. Lindisfarne, by the ebb and flow of the tide, is enclosed twice a day, and twice a day becomes one with the land. There Aidan was often visited by the King, who had made his realm greater than any of his ancestors.

But though raised to so much power Oswald always remained humble, kind, and generous to the poor and to strangers. Bede gives one instance of his almsgiving: "Oswald was sitting at dinner one holy Eastertide, with Aidan by his side. A silver dish was brought and placed before the King. On it were many dainties. Grace was said, and all were about to begin the meal, when a servant in haste came to tell Oswald that a great multitude of poor folk from all parts was sitting in the streets, begging alms of the King. Immediately the King took up the great silver dish, and, giving it to his servant, ordered it to be carried to the poor, and the contents divided among them, and the dish to be broken and distributed." Aidan's eyes were wet with tears as he said: "May this hand never decay!" and he touched the right hand that had given food to God's poor. "This fell

out according to his prayer," says Venerable Bede, "for
his hands with his arms being cut off from his body,
when he was slain in battle, remain uncorrupted to this
day, and are kept in a silver shrine as revered relics in St.
Peter's Church in the royal city." Alas! those precious
relics have been long since destroyed.

King Oswald died, in his thirty-eighth year, on the
battlefield. The place of the battle is probably Oswestry
in Shropshire.   Great miracles connected with his
relics are related by Bede as having taken place to show
how dear to God was Oswald the King. There is only
room for one pretty story. The Queen of the Mercians,
Osthryth, niece of Oswald, wanted very much to
have her uncle's relics venerated in the monastery of
Bardeney. But the monks of that place did not care
to receive the relics; they did not care to have an alien
in their sanctuary. So they left the blessed body out
in the open air all night, only covering it with a tent,
and not having it guarded by anyone, nor honoured
by lights or watching. "But it was revealed by a sign
from Heaven with how much reverence they ought to
be received by all the faithful, for all that night a pillar
of light, reaching from the waggon up to Heaven, was
seen in almost every part of the province of Lindsey.
Thereupon all that monastery began most earnestly to
beg that those holy relics beloved of God might rest
among them. . . . And that there might be a perpetual
memorial of this holy man, they hung up over the
monument his banner of gold and purple." "Nor need

we wonder," says Bede, "that the prayers of that King who is now reigning with Our Lord should be very efficacious with Him, since he, while yet governing the earthly kingdom, was always wont to pray and labour more for that which is eternal. Nay, it is said that he often continued in prayer from the hour of morning thanksgiving (3 a.m.) till it was day." Oswald died as he lived. When his little army was being cut to pieces by his enemies he incessantly prayed: "Lord, have mercy on their souls!" And the words became a proverb.

THE GRIDIRON

St. Lawrence, August 10

THERE IS in Spain, up a height of more than 3,000 feet, a dark grey, granite-built edifice. Its shape resembles a gridiron, and it is dedicated to St. Lawrence. The palace is called the "Escorial," and is the burying-place of many of the Kings of Spain.

Now, the connection between the gridiron-shaped building and St. Lawrence is, of course, this—but perhaps I had better tell the story from the beginning, in case some of you do not know it.

Lawrence was a young man, ordained deacon by St. Sixtus, Pope. There were then seven deacons belonging to the Church of Rome, as there were in Jerusalem in the first ages. Of these seven deacons Lawrence was the head. His office was to distribute the alms of the faithful to the poor of Rome. Lawrence loved the poor, and served them with great charity. I don't know any way by which he could have prepared himself better for martyrdom. He was living in the reign of Valerian, the Roman Emperor. The young deacon loved Sixtus, his father in Christ, more than anything on earth, and he was loved by the venerable Pontiff. When he was led out to die Lawrence met him on the road, and gently upbraided him for going so long a journey without his faithful disciple. "Father, where are you going without your son?" he asked. "You were never used to offer sacrifice without me, your deacon. Have I displeased you? Try me now, and see whether you have made use of a fit minister." "I do not leave you, my son," Sixtus answered; "but a greater trial and a more glorious victory are reserved for you, who are young." Then the Holy Father gave him minute orders about the treasure of the Church. The greedy Roman officials would most certainly come and search for plunder, and carry away all the money and wealth that had been given for the poor. Lawrence, then, must lose no time in distributing all before the robbers came.

The young deacon was filled with joy at the words of the Pope; he was to suffer martyrdom in three days, a glorious martyrdom for his Lord and Master. Without a moment's delay he collected together all the plate, the jewels and the money that had been given by devout Christians for the service of the altar; then he visited the houses of the poor, the orphans, widows, and helpless persons, and gave away all, even to the smallest coin.

No sooner was Sixtus dead than all happened as he had foretold. Officers were sent to Lawrence to demand of him for the Imperial coffers the vast wealth of the Church. It was needed, the prefect said, for the service of the Empire, to maintain just wars, and to keep up the colonies. Lawrence showed no surprise or hesitation. By all means would he collect together all the riches of the Church. The prefect was right, too; the wealth was enormous, beyond price. He must, however, have three days to amass it; let the prefect return at the end of that time, and all should be in readiness. The prefect went away wonderfully elated. He had not expected so easy a victory, and he saw himself already a wealthy man.

Lawrence smiled to himself, too, and set about fulfilling his promise. Once more he made his rounds, and invited together all the sick, the lame, the diseased, the poor, the abject, and the miserable to come to his quarters on the third day. At the time appointed they stood in solemn array in the hall of the house—a ghastly sight; an ailing, halting, crippled crowd. The prefect stood aghast. What had this miserable assembly to do with him? He had asked for money, for riches. Lawrence came forward, and, pointing to his beloved poor, told the Roman that these were the treasure of the Church; that all other wealth passed away with time, and was of no account. To gain true riches let the prefect bestow an abundant alms upon them; thus he would draw down God's blessing upon himself and the Empire.

The prefect was beside himself with anger. He turned furiously upon the young deacon. "I know you wish to die; but yours shall be no short, easy death: you shall die by inches in horrible torture." Then a gridiron was made ready, a slow fire was lighted beneath, and

Lawrence was chained to the iron bars. The flames spread slowly; they penetrated the delicate body through and through, but so ardently burnt the love of God in the young martyr's heart that he seemed hardly conscious of the pain. He jested with the executioners; one side was done to a nicety, had they not better turn the other? he said. With his last breath he prayed to God for the conversion of his beloved city—Rome. The Christians standing round saw his face shine as with a Heavenly light; they smelled a sweet odour as of burning incense. When the martyr's victory was won, some noble Romans, who had been witnesses of his cruel death, and who had seen with what constancy and joy he had laid down his life, were converted on the spot, and took what remained of the Saint's body, and carried it reverently to the grave. And this was the beginning of the answer to Lawrence's petition for the conversion of Rome. Does not God bless those who love the poor?

"BROTHER LAETUS"

St. John Berchmans, August 13

Brother Laetus means Brother Joyful. Would you like to know whose nickname that was? You will be rather surprised, perhaps. A boy was called that who had made up his mind from his very young days to be a Saint. Now, many are of opinion that joy and sanctity are rather hard to be thought of together. But that's their mistake, and the life of St. John Berchmans explains it. His feast is kept on August 13, because he died on that day, just in time to be in Heaven for our dear Lady's Assumption. And he did love Our Lady, and she loved him.

John had a beautiful face, and his beauty was made more expressive because his eyes were lit up with this joy that made him to be called Brother Laetus. When a little fellow he used to play ball with all his heart; when he came to the Jesuit noviceship he played games whenever he was asked to, and when he played he gave his whole mind to the game. He would not talk of other things, nor would he look about him. Of course, if he lost he was never upset, because that is never worth while, but he looked pleased if he won.

He was what we should call a poor boy. His father was a shoemaker of Diest, but he held many honourable posts in his native town. All the same, he was not rich, and often he thought he would have to take his eldest boy away from his studies to put him to some trade that would bring in money. John wanted to be a priest, so he used to beg his father on his knees not to take him away from college. He promised to live cheaply and earn his college fees by doing some work. So the good father consented, and John went to Mechlin and lived in the house of a Canon, who learnt to love him as if he had been his son. He gave him charge of two little boys who lived in his house as boarders. John was like an angel guardian to these little fellows. He said morning and night prayers with them, dressed and undressed them, and taught them their lessons. For this duty John was able to stay at college and learn all that was necessary for the priesthood. Children always loved John; when he went about teaching Catechism or telling stories, they liked to listen to him better than to anyone else. So he used to have troops of these small beings following his footsteps, and learning holy things from his lips.

When John was about eighteen he had another call. He felt he must become a Jesuit; he had heard of the great founder, St. Ignatius, of his wonderful Society, of the Saints that had lived in it—Aloysius and Stanislaus. And he thought that with such helps as they had he could become a Saint too. His father was at first much disappointed, for he had hoped that John, his eldest son, would help to look after his younger brothers and sister; but being a very holy man, he gave his permission once more. And God rewarded him, for he became a priest himself.

When all had been arranged John set out on the long journey to Rome with a companion. It was a tremendous journey in those days, and very dangerous, for there were freebooters and half-savage soldiers overrunning Europe at their pleasure. But John was protected by his blessed Mother in Heaven, and arrived safely at the Eternal City. He was very soon quite at home amongst the young scholastics; he was given the very same lamps to trim that the Marquis's son, Aloysius, had cleaned about forty years before. He took upon himself all the disagreeable things he could find. If anyone wanted a companion to go out, Berchmans was called, and though he was studying hard at the time, he always found the means to do a kind service. It was a joy to meet the beautiful boy in the passages, for his smile was gladdening. At recreation John would tell funny stories, and help the conversation to take a happy turn. All in the house loved him. He loved his brothers in religion with true love, and he was loved by them. His mortifications were of such a kind as you and I could imitate. He never leant back in his chair; he knelt without a support for his hands; he ate what came to his portion; he never asked for extras; he was

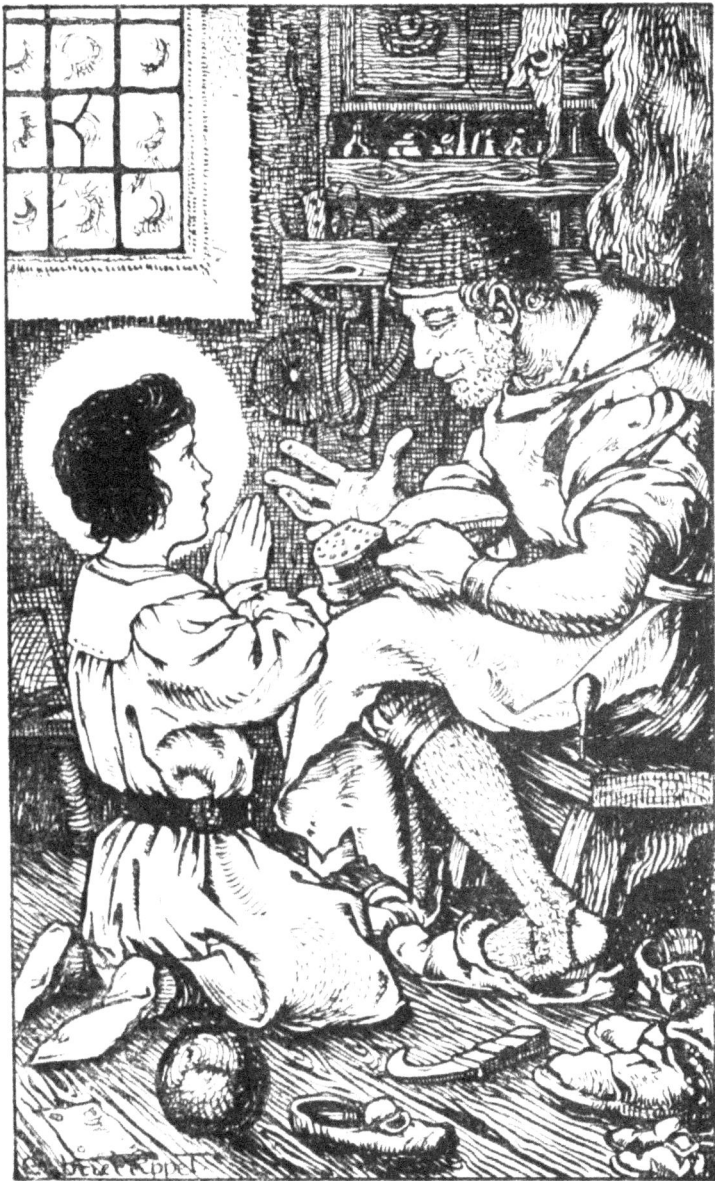

John wants to be a Priest.

content with all, and performed each action as well as he could. "Common life is my mortification," he used to say. Great austerities are not recorded of him. But fidelity in little things made him a Saint.

Do you know how old he was when he came to die? Only twenty-two! Not very old, was he? Yet he had time to make himself, with the grace of God, a Saint. You see, he set out with this thought, "I mean to be a Saint, and a great one!" and he kept on, and became one.

I must tell you of his great act of faith on his death bed. Perhaps you may like to make it when you go to Holy Communion. The Rector held the Blessed Sacrament up in his hands; the room was crowded with brethren; the holy boy was half kneeling, supported by two of the Fathers at each side. Weak and dying as he was, John, in a loud, clear voice, said: "I declare that there is here really present the Son of God the Father, and of the Most Blessed Mary, ever a Virgin. I wish to live and die a true son of our Holy Mother the Catholic, Apostolic, Roman Church; I wish to live and die a true son of the Blessed Virgin Mary; I wish to live and die a true son of the Society." He said a most loving good-bye to all his brothers in Christ. He took them in his arms, and pressed them to him.

Don't you believe people when they tell you that religion starves human love in the heart. Such a thing is impossible and against reason. At the very last, when the Saint could no longer hold up his Rule Book and rosary and crucifix, he propped them against his knees, and died looking at his treasures. Read the life of this dear boy-Saint, John Berchmans, and see if you don't get to love him and imitate him!

ST. TARCISIUS, MARTYR

August 15

SOMETIMES we think we will do great things for God *when we grow up*. We hear of Saints, and confessors, and martyrs who did such wonders—they fasted, and prayed, and suffered, they even died, for God. But then we find that they *were grown up* and we think that that makes all the difference.

But it does not; at least, not *all* the difference. Many, many of the Saints were Saints as little children, and some were martyrs—such babies were martyred in Japan. I know that they had special graces, and special opportunities, and special calls; all I mean is, that it won't do to hug ourselves and think we must wait for *time* to make us good and holy. We shall have to make ourselves—that is, take Our Lord's grace through the Sacraments, through the Mass, through prayer, and turn it to the very best account. We are not offered more cake until we have finished the piece on our plate, and if we are, we have the self-denial generally to refuse it until we have finished.

Something like that goes on with grace—that wonderful gift of God without which we can do nothing for our salvation. It is ready waiting until the first grace offered is worked up; then a second and a third are given. And as we use them we get more and more holy, and rise higher, and get nearer to God, and become Saints indeed.

Still, God has His favourites, and He does seem to pour down grace upon some when they are very small. Have you read about Tarcisius, the martyr? Let me tell you over again, if you have; the story bears retelling.

The terrible persecution under Valentinian and Galienus was raging. It was about the middle of the third century, and the Church was suffering much. Her priests were few and well known. There was much work to be done, and few to do it. So it became a custom to allow the faithful to take home with them the most Holy Sacrament of the Altar. See how necessary these first Christians thought Our Lord was to them! When they were imprisoned the first thought of their friends was to bring them the Holy Eucharist, and if they could not find a priest, they made use of a deacon, or even a layman, to carry the precious Food.

One day there were prisoners famished for this Heavenly Food, and no one could be found to take It to them. At last a boy called Tarcisius was entrusted with the treasure. He folded the sacred Species in his robe, and carried It through the crowded Roman streets. An idle mob lay in his way, bent on wicked fun. They saw the boy, and called out to him to show what he carried so warily. The child hurried forward; far too precious was his burden for such uninstructed folk. But they were not to be balked; his quick going added excitement to their curiosity. They pursued him down the narrow lanes, and when they saw he was determined not to surrender, they took up stones and flung them at him. Others, nearer, struck him with their thick, knobbed sticks.

The boy reeled and dropped, still clinging to his sacred trust. There was a cry; the mob fell upon him, and sought among his garments for his treasure. They found nothing! With a parting kick of disgust they left the mangled body. The boy was taken up by some Christians passing by, and there on his breast lay, in sight of all, the Sacred Host he had died to save!

Tarcisius was buried in the cemetery of St. Callistus on August 15, and a great Pope had inscribed upon his grave the words: "Tarcisius, carrying the Sacraments of Christ, chose rather to suffer death than to betray the Heavenly Body."

That was a brave boy, was it not? We feel so afraid sometimes when people speak angrily or threaten things, even when we know they can't do them; and here is one who would not give up his trust though he was pursued to the death.

Another story:

A Jewish boy at Constantinople went to school with Christian boys. He used to hear of their going up to the altar rails to receive the sacred fragments that were left after all had received Holy Communion. And he longed to be with them, and receive Our Lord too. So one day, without saying anything to anyone, he crept up to the rails, and knelt with the rest. He returned to his place and prayed with the greatest devotion. But his father got to hear of what he, a Jewish boy, had done. He was mad with rage, and determined to kill the boy. He caught him by the shoulder, and flung him into the furnace, which was glowing at red heat.

The poor mother knew nothing of this wicked deed, and looked in vain for her child. He was nowhere to be found; no one knew anything of his hiding-place. At last she heard his voice come, as it were, from under the furnace. Horror-struck, she opened the door. But there, quite unharmed, crouched the little fellow. He explained that a beautiful Lady had kept off the hot air of the flames from him, and had whispered sweet things in his ear. Soon after, mother and son were baptized, and both were able to receive Our Lord publicly; for the Emperor Justinian heard their story, and took them under his protection.

BLESSED IMELDA

IT WAS about the year 1322 that Imelda Lambertini
was born. Her name means in Latin "Go, give
honey," and the little child really received and gave
spiritually the true "honey" in a very wonderful manner.
She was the child who, by her great longing, brought
Our Lord from His tabernacle-home to her side in
Holy Communion.

Imelda, when a little child, lived in a convent. She
went to church and to Mass like the nuns; she saw them
going to Holy Communion every day, and she longed
to go too. One day she told the Sisters how strong
her longing was, and begged them to let her receive
her Lord. Now, in those days it was not customary for
children to make their First Communion very young,
and the good nuns did not like to make an exception for
Imelda. So the poor child had to watch the Sisters go
up to the holy table, and come away filled with all good
things, and remain herself hungry with a great hunger.
But little Imelda was wise. What man would not give
her she determined to ask from God Himself. So she

prayed with all her heart to Our Lord to let her receive Him into her heart. It was after Mass on the eve of the Ascension. The nuns had left the chapel, but Imelda knelt on. Suddenly a glorious light shone about her, and the Sacred Host hovered over her head. Someone saw the miracle, and called the chaplain. He waited reverently with the paten in his hand. The Sacred Host rested upon it, and the priest gave the child the Bread of Life. In awe and wonder the community waited by the child's side, joining with her in fervent acts of adoration and love. When one of the Sisters went to rouse her, she found the child had gone Home; the joy of that First Communion was too great for her little human heart. It had broken with joy, and left her free to go to Our Lord for ever.

Was not Imelda a happy little child! But are not little children happy nowadays? No one can keep them from Our Lord; so long as they *know* the Divine Bread and so long as they are free from sin, they may come even daily to Communion. And many, many little ones do know this Bread, and do keep free from sin, and are growing up daily and becoming daily more and more one with Our Lord according to His burning desire. How many of my children, my little readers, I wonder, are daily communicants! How I long to know that the dear Holy Father's wish is being carried out in more and more homes, the wish that little ones should come to Our Lord and receive Him daily into their hearts! Draw near, little ones, and see how good, how loving

He is, and how much He loves you! It is only by being much with a person that you get to love him much. Come and be much with this Divine Lord, and He will build you up and form your characters, and mould you to do His will. Pray to little Imelda, who found out so early Who the Blessed Sacrament is, that she may obtain for you a great love of the Blessed Sacrament of the Altar.

A HERO, SAINT, AND KING

St. Louis, August 25

YOU ALL have learnt about Richard Cœur de Lion and about John Sansterre. But probably you did not notice that in their genealogy there is an Eleanor, sister to these two Kings. This Eleanor married Alphonsus of Castile, the warrior King who marched against and conquered 200,000 Moors. Eleanor's little daughter was Blanche of Castile, the wife of Louis VIII of France.

Perhaps you are wondering what I am coming to with all this history talk. Well, it just amounts to this. I want to show that my hero, Saint, and King, Louis IX of France, is some connection of ours; that we could have him in a well-worked-out genealogy—and that is a satisfaction to me. Louis was grand-nephew to the knight-errant Richard and the worthless John; in his childhood he may have heard his grandmother relate the exploits of Cœur de Lion on the Crusade, thus making him long to do and dare something for the love of the Holy Land.

Blanche was a good mother. She was left Regent of the kingdom by the early death of her husband, and she reigned worthily. Louis was but twelve when his royal father died; he well repaid his mother's care, for he became a model ruler and a Saint.

When you can, read Joinville's Memoirs of Louis IX. Joinville was the greatest man in the kingdom after the King, and he loved him with all his soul. He tells all about his doings and his sayings; he accompanied him on the first Crusade; he sat by him when he gave judgment under the spreading oak; he saw his kindness to the poor, his sternness to the wicked, his compassion for the unfortunate. One time he heard him order a wealthy man, who was a blasphemer, to be branded on the mouth, to teach him to use his lips aright. Some blamed the King for ordering so terrible a punishment. Louis was surprised. "Why," he said, "I would willingly be branded to prevent such an outrage." Another man he fined so heavily that he lost almost all he possessed, because he had hanged three children for hunting rabbits. The money was employed to found Masses for the children's souls.

Joinville saw the King cool and composed when bad news was brought to him. Once two assassins were found ready to murder Louis. He sent them courteously back to the master who had paid them. Again, Joinville, sitting at the Council Board with the young King, listened to his wise sayings. Things of worldwide importance were discussed, and Louis took part in all that was said. "He has the wisest and best head in the Council" was Joinville's opinion.

A monarch made Louis a great present once. He brought him the crown of thorns from the Holy Land. Louis loved Our Lord with all his heart, and he was beside himself with joy at this most holy relic. How could he honour it enough? was his thought. To this very day we know how the great King honoured the sacred crown. He built for it the most beautiful chapel that exists, one that you can see when you go to Paris, for it remains still to show the people of France how their greatest King reverenced the Passion of Our Lord.

Louis IX was no carpet knight. He could fight and win, and when he heard of the horrors that were being wrought in the Holy Land, he went to the church of St. Denis, and took the Oriflamme, the blessed standard of France, and set out for Palestine. He sailed from Aigues Mortes with his three brothers, his wife, and 120 large vessels, and numberless smaller ones. On board there were over 1,200 knights, and more than three times as many picked soldiers. Louis fought like a hero, and was admired by his very foe for his prowess and his splendid honour. But he was taken a prisoner, and in chains won his enemies' admiration a thousandfold more. "Never did we see so proud a Christian," they said. By "proud" they meant one who held to his own principles, who stood his ground, and commanded their respect. They sought to terrify the King by an exhibition of racks and torturing machines. But he looked at them without concern. Their threats to punish and bruise and crush him brought no pallor to his face. Simply because he knew his fate was in God's hands, and without His consent they could do him no harm.

A second time Louis sailed for the dear East. He stayed at Damietta, and caught the fever that was striking down hundreds of his men. For twenty days he burned with the fever of his disease, and then his end came. He was in a tent outside Damietta, in the stifling heat; but never a murmur escaped his lips. On the day of his death, about twelve o'clock, he raised his eyes to Heaven, and said: "I will enter into Thy holy house, I will adore towards Thy holy temple, O Lord !" At three he spoke again: " Into Thy hands I commend my spirit." Then the soul of the great hero, King, and Saint went to its eternal Home.

FRIENDS

St.Augustine, August 28

THERE was a young boy called Alipius, who lived at Tagaste, a city of North Africa. He was a clever fellow of good family. His father sent him to Carthage when he grew old enough to learn rhetoric. There he studied for some time under one Augustine, a professor, and a very learned young man, with whom he became fast friends. Alipius loved the shows of the circus; he wasted his time and worse in watching the games until he was warned by Augustine that such ways were bad. Now Augustine himself was by no means a Saint at this time. Indeed, he tells us himself that his young friend was by far the better; he at least kept himself pure and loved virtue, whilst Augustine gave himself up to all kinds of pleasure. The two friends both joined a wicked sect called Manicheans, and because they did not pray, lowered their fine intellects until they were even able to believe there are two gods, a good and a bad one.

One day Alipius was in great danger; he was seen with a stolen hatchet, and without inquiry was taken off to prison as though he were a thief. It was a little child who told of his innocence, and proved it. This incident made Alipius see how dangerous it is to judge people rashly.

Though Alipius loved the shows of the circus, he could not bear to see gladiators fight. He would never go to the amphitheatre at Rome for this reason. One day, however, his friends clustered round him, and begged him to accompany them just once. He need not look, they said, if he was so squeamish; he need only entertain them during the intervals. Alipius was very good-natured, and did not like to seem disobliging. So, unhappily, he yielded, and went to the amphitheatre. He sat with his friends, but resolutely shut his eyes or watched the gay figures in the seats around. Suddenly there was a scream, then a prolonged shout and excited cries. Alipius looked. One of the fighters was lying wounded on the ground; the blood flowed freely, his face was white and drawn, his lips purple. Alipius, far from being sickened with the sight, was fascinated. He watched, he applauded louder even than the others, his soul seemed intoxicated with the combat; and when he went away it was with the determination of returning at the first opportunity. And he did, and often brought others with him to see the horrible spectacle. Nor was this enough ; all his former love of the circus returned too, so that the one thought in his mind was brutal pleasure.

Would you not be inclined to say: "All is up with that young man now. Far from becoming better, he has gone back, and lost everything"? That is just what you and I must never say of another, nor even of ourselves. As long as we have life we can repent and do better. When we have fallen we must get up and go on again. No matter how many are the falls or how comfortable is the sitting, we must rise and get up again.

Just think of Alipius. He was degraded enough to love cruel, murder-like sport! He could watch a fellow-man die, and applaud as if it were a game. Yet he became a Bishop and a Saint. He had been a member of one of the lowest sects of heretics, and he became a great defender of the Faith; he had wasted his time shamefully, and he became a priest, and consecrated himself and all that he had to God.

As the two friends grew older their friendship grew stronger; wherever Augustine went Alipius followed. From Tagaste they went to Rome; from there to Milan. There the two learnt to know the great Ambrose, Bishop of the city; and there God spoke to their hearts. They were baptized together, and did penance together in solitude and quiet. They shared all they had. Augustine's mother, Monica, was his friend's mother too; her house was Alipius's home; their books and studies were all in common. The two became Saints together, and encouraged each other to every virtue.

St. Jerome, the great Latin Doctor of the Church, was living at Bethlehem then. Both Saints visited him at different times, and both loved and admired him. Augustine told him of his friend, and said: "Anyone who knows us would say that he and I are only two in body, not in soul."

There is tremendous strength in such a friendship, and tremendous help either for good or evil. Thank God, the friendship of these two men turned for good. No one could have said at one time that Augustine could help anyone. Wise parents would have said: "Keep away from that sinner; he can only do you harm." Yet that sinner became a most wonderful Saint, and helped his friend to become one also. And he has been the pattern and the consolation of all real penitents from then till now.

SEPTEMBER

"FORMIDABLE AS AN ARMY IN BATTLE ARRAY"

Holy Name of Mary, September 12

Our Lady's birthday is on September 8. The feast of her holy name is kept on the Sunday within the octave. You would hardly think it, but there is a great battle connected with this feast, or rather the feast was instituted because of the battle and victory. I will tell you the story of it, and you will see how good Our Lady is to those who come to her for help.

About the year 1683 there had been a terrible insurrection in Hungary. The people had rebelled against the Emperor Leopold, and had even called in the Turks to help them in their wars. You may imagine how very pleased the Turks would be to help anybody if they could get a foot into such a fine land as Germany. The case is very like that of our Britons and Saxons.

Well, Cara Mustaph, Grand Vizier of Mahomet IV, hung up the horse-tails outside his tent at Adrianople. These horse-tails were a signal for war, and when the citizens saw the sign they prepared for battle. The cry went up that fire and sword were to be carried into the German Empire; there was to be plunder and licence, and wealth for the taking. So the horde spread through Hungary, on, on towards Vienna. Cara passed the little town of Raab, but left it alone—too insignificant, they thought, to bother about it. This was a mistake; it is a rule of war never to leave a fortress untaken on the route. When the hot sun of July was burning, the Turks laid siege to Vienna. They pitched their camp round the walls, and a fearful sight it was. The siege began on July 4. Tekeli, the Hungarian rebel, conducted it in person. The infidels burnt the suburbs and attacked the fortifications. These were poor enough, but they were defended with wonderful skill and energy. Nevertheless, the city was doomed unless help from outside could be obtained. All Europe trembled. If Vienna fell, not only was Germany open to the enemy, but the whole of the Continent. In this strait Pope Innocent XI made a league, and the principal ally was the renowned Sobieski, King John of Poland. The Poles were feared by the Turks more than any other nation. They had conquered them in many battles, and alone had kept them at bay. So John with 24,000 men marched towards Vienna. They occupied the mountains around, and took a castle near. Sobieski was a hero; he could fight and conquer; he could rest and march. But above all he could pray, and Vienna was saved by prayer. It was the King's custom to serve Mass himself. On the eve of the battle he prayed with his arms outstretched and received Holy Communion. When the Mass was over he said in a firm voice: "Let us go to the enemy with an entire confidence in the Blessed Virgin."

The attack was to be made upon the Grand Vizier's own quarters. Mustapha was in his tent with his two sons and some officers. News was brought to them of the advance of the Christian army. But Mustapha was so confident in his own skill and in the fidelity of his troops that he merely laughed, and continued drinking his coffee with the utmost indifference. The only precaution he took was to order a detachment to set out for the castle near at hand; but a whole regiment was kept by his side, calmly watching the advancing army. Hill after hill was taken by the Poles, and the men fell in hundreds. Still he lingered. At last Mustapha heard that the great Sobieski was himself at the head of his troops; a panic seized the infidel, and he fled without a blow. When the sun was setting, when the church bells rang six, King John entered Vienna, and went at once to the Cathedral to give thanks for his wonderful victory. Immense riches fell into the hands of the Christians. The great standard taken from before the

tent of Cara Mustapha was sent to the Holy Father.
Another standard was hung up in the principal church
of Vienna. Only 600 Christian soldiers fell during this
terrible day. To thank Our Lady for her protection, the
Holy Father ordered the Feast of the Holy Name of
Mary to be instituted. Let us imitate the great Sobieski
in his love for and confidence in Our Lady. We shall
find that work goes much better when we pray. "Soak
your work in prayer, and see what a difference it will
make!"

THE DWARF SAINT

St. John Colobus, September 15

THERE was a child once who, at eight years of age, was so small that she was always called *Tiny*. Now, Tiny had one great fear in her heart, and it was so big a fear that she did not dare tell anyone—which was, and is always, a stupid policy to adopt. She feared that she was a *dwarf*, and she was afraid that if she asked about it she would most certainly be told she was. And Tiny thought that to fear you're a dwarf is very bad, but to know you are a dwarf is far worse. So she grew up to be quite an elderly girl before she dared to say anything about her size. Then she was told that she was not a dwarf at all, and not particularly noticeable in any way.

When Tiny grew bigger still, and was called by her own proper name, she wondered over these fears, and it came to her mind that even dwarfs can serve God quite well, and lame people, too, and the dear blind and the deaf. So it would not have really mattered so frightfully if she had been a dwarf.

Now, John the Dwarf must have felt like that from the beginning, for we never hear that he was troubled about his smallness. He simply served God, and served Him so very well that he became a Saint. And I am going to tell you something about his life. It is so wonderful that you will perhaps be inclined to think that it was all a queer mistake. But there you would be very wrong, and quite silly. Saints are philosophers, and the way they gain their end is very much alike. For instance, there was a pagan philosopher once who was teaching at Athens. A young man asked to be allowed to attend the lectures. The wise man told him to go and break stones with the prisoners for three years. The young man obeyed, and returned. The wise man then told him to pay someone to insult him daily, and to bear the insults without a word. The young man obeyed again. "Now," said the philosopher, "you are fit for my school. Go to Athens and study." At the gate of the city sat an old man who made it his business to revile all who passed him by. When the young novice passed that way the old man began his abuse. But the boy laughed at him, and on being asked how he could laugh at such insults, said that he might well laugh, for hitherto he had paid men to abuse him, and here he found one ready to abuse him for nothing.

The philosopher of Athens wanted his disciple to learn perfect self-command, and that is why he kept him under submission, and put him to such hard trials. The Saints have such-like ways too. John the Dwarf went into the desert with his elder brother to learn the wisdom of the Saints. His first master commanded

He watered it for three years.

him to water a dry stick for three years. John watered it without a murmur, though the water was far to fetch and the stick very dry. But at the end of the three years the stick bore beautiful green leaves and blossom and fruit. And beautiful as the fruit was, much more beautiful was John's soul, I am sure. The wise people of this world laugh sometimes when they hear of the trials undergone by the Saints. But these wise men set their pupils trials quite as laborious and lengthy as any undergone by the Saints. Men say of mathematics, or science, or classics, which take years to learn, that it is not necessarily the knowledge that matters, but that the practice of the science, etc., is such a good discipline for the mind. So the Saints argued about *their* science.

But John was very young when he first determined to be a Saint, and like all young people he made mistakes. One day he said to his brother: "I could wish to live without all concern of earthly things, and be a Saint wholly given up to contemplation." So saying, he left his cloak behind with his brother, and went far away into the desert. After a week's absence, he knocked at his brother's door. The brother from within asked the visitor's name.

"John!" answered the youth.

"John! How can that be? My brother John has become an angel, and no longer lives among men."

But poor John opened the door, and confessed that he could not lay aside all earthly concerns, that he must eat and drink like a human being.

John could not bear gossip, and used rather to snub those who came merely to talk of the weather. But he could talk without ceasing about God and holy things. One day a friend of his, a hermit, came to speak a few words to John. They began to talk on spiritual matters, and instead of a few minutes they stayed together till early morning, passing the whole night in holy conversation. Seeing the morning sun in the heavens, John went a few steps on the way with his friend. But midday found them still together, so they had to turn back once more and break their fast in each other's company.

There is a great deal more to say about this simple man who was a dwarf. But we must stop, with the big wish that you and I may learn to follow the things of God as the wise Saints did.

THE LEGEND OF THE THEBAN LEGION

St. Maurice & Companions, September 22

A LEGION was a Roman regiment; not, as a little girl said, "things you wear on your legs." She meant leggings, of course, which are quite different. This legion was called Theban, probably because it came from the neighbourhood of the old city of Thebes, of which we hear so much in ancient Greek history. How the legion was converted to the Christian Faith we do not know. But in the time of Maximin, Emperor of Rome, the soldiers were Christians. Some think that a holy Bishop of Jerusalem converted them. That may be, but there is no certainty about the fact.

This legion was ordered from the East to Gaul; they were to be stationed on the Lake of Geneva. The head of the regiment was a young man called Maurice, a noble, brave, loyal soldier, honoured and respected by his companions and trusted by his superiors.

One day the order came from headquarters that the Christians of the district were to be put to death by the soldiery. Maurice heard the command. He had never disobeyed an order in his life before. Obedience came like a second nature to him. But here was an order in direct opposition to his conscience, to the law of God. Not one moment did he waver. God or the King? God must conquer. Maurice proclaimed himself a Christian, and refused to obey. With one voice the 6,000 repeated the refusal. They had risked their lives many a time in the service of Cæsar. But then their bodies only were at stake. Now it was a question of the soul, and that belonged to God, their Supreme Master.

It is a terrible thing when soldiers rebel. They are the bulwark of the State; they bear the arms, they command the sources of a nation's safety. If they turn their strength and experience against the mother that has nurtured and drilled them it is a desperate case indeed. Maurice, the good soldier, must have felt an extreme repugnance to mutiny; but the choice lay between God and man, and his soul could know no hesitation.

His refusal and that of his legion was told to the Emperor, and the decree was issued that the legion should be decimated over and over again. Do you know what that means? Every tenth man was to be put to death. So the brave soldiers stood in their ranks, and the counting began.

Without a murmur, without the slightest sign of violence, the 6,000 waited for their turn. There was no flinching, there was no renegade. All, in good order, with perfect patience laid down their heads on the block, and lost their lives to find them in a happy eternity. The place where those brave men fell is still called after the gallant leader, and they are honoured throughout all time as holy Christian martyrs.

Do you know I have a great love for soldiers? Of course, I know they have their faults—we could all count them off on our fingers—but haven't they virtues, too? Are they not always ready to march, to suffer, to fight, to die? If they are real soldiers they are. And I wonder which of us is so ready to do hard things. I do not feel at all so sure of myself, but then, of course, it is only me. Other civilians may feel just as brave and self-sacrificing as any soldiers, but sometimes I doubt it.

OCTOBER

ST. FRANCIS'S SERMON TO THE BIRDS

St. Francis of Assisi, October 4

PERHAPS some of you think that is rather a funny title to give a story. You have heard of sermons at missions in the open air, but they were given to people, not to birds. Well, I will tell you how it came about that the birds got a sermon all to themselves.

There was a great Saint once called St. Francis of Assisi; and he loved all creatures, big and little, because they were God's creatures. One day this Saint was preaching in a small town called Saverniano. He was out in the open air, and the swallows were twittering in the trees. St. Francis turned to them and told them they must be silent until he had done preaching, for he could not hear his own voice, so noisy were they. The swallows stopped immediately, and not another sound did they make till the sermon was over.

Now, whether this obedience pleased the Saint very much, or whether it made him think that he would like to speak to such docile creatures, I don't know. But as he was turning down the road he saw some trees filled with birds of all kinds. So he went into a field where trees were growing and began to preach. Then there was a soft rustling and a swish of feathers; down the birds came from every bough, and gathered round him in silent clusters. They looked up into his face, stretched out their wings, and opened their beaks, and listened with great reverence. When the sermon was over the birds still waited upon the ground without a movement, until St. Francis raised his hand and blessed them with a large sign of the Cross; then they burst out singing, filling the air with joyous song, filling the hearts of men with their own gladness. As they rose high in the air they parted into four companies—some went north, some south, some east, some west—and as they flew they sang their wondrous songs, making, as it were, a cross of melody in the air.

St. Francis stood and watched them and listened, and he thanked God for the beauty of birds, for their sweet simplicity, their joyous song, and their attentive listening.

Now, I wonder if any of you would like to know what the birds heard. I am thinking that if the birds could listen to it, you could. It is only a little sermon, so it will just suit you. "My little sisters the birds," it began, "you are bound to give much praise to God your Creator, because He preserved you in the ark from being drowned, because He feeds you, and clothes you, and gives you rivers, and mountains, and high trees for your nests. Therefore, my little sisters the birds, beware of the sin of ingratitude, and try always to give praise to God." It was those words, "give praise to God," that made the little birds sing so joyously, I think, because it is by the right kind of joyousness that we praise God best. Birds and children have a good many things in common, I fancy. They have not to think much of clothes or food or drink—at least the very young ones haven't—and they sing, too, generally. Now, wouldn't it be nice for them to praise God like these Italian birds? They would help grown-ups, who have so much to think of, to praise God, too, as St. Francis did when he saw and heard that joyous flock near Saverniano.

VANITY OF VANITIES!

St. Francis Borgia, October 11

IF YOU want to read the life of a Saint that is as interesting as any story, and a great deal more interesting than most, I advise you to get the life of St. Francis Borgia. His feast is kept on October 11. From his babyhood to his death it is full of incident and romance. I am only going to tell you of one event, and I have chosen this one because it had the greatest consequences in his after-life.

Francis, the son of the Duke of Gandia, was a beautiful boy. He was brought up at Court, and taught everything that a young grandee ought to know; he learnt his Catechism, and said it upon his knees, and at seven used to teach his little pages to serve at Mass. At one time he thought he would like to be a priest, or a religious, so his father, in order to make him stay in the world, sent him to the Emperor's Court. There he lived a brilliant life, taking part in hawking and hunting, and all the diversions that such a life offered. The Emperor, Charles V, was very fond of the young noble. They studied mathematics together, travelled together, and transacted business together. For fear of being led into sin through idleness and waste of time, Francis learnt music. He played on several instruments and sang well. Throughout his whole life this great man kept himself pure from sin. He never gambled, nor would he even watch those who played, and he prayed like a religious.

Time went on, and Francis married; he had eight children, and he was very happy. Yet he seemed always to think that he was meant for greater things than worldly goodness and happiness. And it was true; God was waiting His time. The Empress Isabella, Charles's wife, and a friend of Francis's, died. Francis, as one of the greatest nobles of Spain, was ordered to accompany her body to Granada, and never to leave the coffin on the way. He faithfully fulfilled his mournful task. When he reached Granada, the leaden coffin was to be opened, and the Duke was to swear that the body within was that of the beautiful Empress, the admired of all the Courts of Europe.

The hour came. Francis was in readiness. The workmen did their work. The heavy leaden lid was lifted away, and there was opened to the terrified gaze of courtiers, pages, and priests an awful spectacle of human corruption. The room was filled with the frightful odour; the lovely face was unrecognizable. Francis stood by, awestruck and dumb. Over and over again he asked himself could this be the mistress whom he had served with such chivalrous devotion: "Are you her sacred Majesty? are you my lady and mistress?"

he murmured. He could not take the oath as to the remains, he said at last. There was no vestige there of the renowned Sovereign whose every feature he knew. He could only swear that, according to order, he had never left the coffin.

For thirty-three years that awful sight haunted the holy man. It had brought home to him what before was only like a dim truth, that all the world can offer is vanity of vanity, lasting so short a time as to be of no account.

As soon as the holy Duke could lay aside his crown and his duties, he entered the Society of Jesus, and became a scullion in their kitchens, a servant about their holy halls, and in the end, the third General of their Order. Or, rather, in the end, a canonized Saint of the Church.

But, dear children, get the book of the Saint's life. This is only one little story, and there are many more, and much to be learnt from each.

THE SAINT AND THE ROBBERS

St. John Cantius, October 20

JOHN Cantius was a Saint. He lived at the beginning of the fifteenth century. I'm going to tell you a little story about him. And as I tell it, I imagine that you who are reading it fall into two classes. There may be a lot of divisions in the classes, but there will be mainly two classes. In the one there will be those who think the Saint a simpleton, and nothing more or less; and in the other those who admire the simplicity as being of the Kingdom of Heaven. Of course, I am not going to say on which side I am; that is my business. But the shrewd readers will guess, I think.

Well, John Cantius was going to Rome one day, when, like the Israelite, he fell among robbers. They flung him down, and demanded all his money. John gave up all he had, and told them he had no more. They let him go his way, and they went theirs. As John recovered his breath and his presence of mind, he remembered that he had stowed away a few gold pieces. He was horrified to think that he had told an untruth and deceived the robbers. So he hastened after them, knelt down, and confessed his fault, and handed to them the precious gold pieces.

Now see what happened. The robbers were so much taken aback at the Saint's simplicity that they returned to him all the money they had taken, and humbly begged his pardon!

If we take this story to pieces we shall see that the dear, simple Saint had nothing to be sorry about. He had said what was not true, but he had not told a lie. For a lie is an intentional unjust keeping back of the truth. In John's case it was a mere lapse of the memory. So really there was no matter for contrition even. Again, suppose he had really told a lie, then he would have had to be sorry for it, but there was not the slightest occasion for the presentation of the gold pieces to the plunderers. By his statement he had deprived them of unlawful gains, but by no reasoning could they have had a right to his money.

Still—on which side are you? Was John a simpleton? Or was he simple with the simplicity that wins Heaven? It is evident what the robbers thought.

NOVEMBER

GIVING

St. Martin of Tours, November 11

THERE are many ways of giving. I have seen a picture of a country lad surrounded by a group of companions. The middle boy has cheeks like apples, and a rosy apple in his hand. He is the hero of the group for the moment because of this possession, and he is just going to give a bite to a friend. But just watch the precautions he takes. I dare say a village lad could take a desperate bite out of even a big apple, but this boy is not going to be allowed to. The owner has clenched his two hands round the fruit, leaving only the smallest round of shining red left for the boy to get at; and while the poor fellow strives to bite, the donor eyes him with starting orbs and flushing cheeks.

Very different was the way of a little girl I knew. She used to keep all her sweets till her sisters and brothers had finished theirs. Then she would produce them, and

distribute them all round with as much pleasure as if
their feasting were hers too.

Different, again, was the giving of some rowdy young
fellows. They were seated in a balcony overlooking a
crowd of sightseers standing in the street below. It was
a badly-dressed crowd, dwellers in the neighbouring
slums. The young fellows were up to a lark, as they would
probably have explained. They dropped halfpence on
the poor people under their window. A scrambling and
a fighting ensued. Then yells of pain and anger. The
coins were red hot!

Some give begrudgingly, some generously, some
cruelly. We will have nothing to do with the mean or
cruel ways of giving, but as this week we keep the feast
of dear St. Martin of Tours, soldier and Bishop, I will
tell you how the Saints give.

A brilliant squadron of soldiers in shining armour
and bright red military cloaks was pressing towards the
town of Amiens. The air was bitterly cold; a cutting
wind swept across the plain; the breath froze on the
hairy lips of the soldiers. They wrapped themselves
more closely round, and beat their breasts to circulate
their blood; for they had seen dead bodies lying on the
road, frozen with the unusual bitterness of the winter.
At the city gate there shivered a beggar; his trembling
hand was reaching out for alms, his lips were blue, the
finger-tips black. But the young men rode on in careless
selfishness, only too anxious to reach the comparatively
warm quarters of their barracks. One by one they went
by in their strength and insolence. Among the last to

pass was Martin, a catechumen, a boy who was learning the Christian religion, but who was not yet a soldier of Christ. He noticed the miserable object at his feet, and pitied his grey hairs. But what had he to give? His pockets were empty; gold and silver he had none. A light crossed his mind: the man was shivering; he must be clad. Martin swung off his brilliant cloak, folded it in two, took out his sword, and cut the cloak in a clean half. Stooping low in the saddle, he handed the warm woollen garment to the astonished beggar, and then galloped after his comrades. He was greeted with laughter. "A fine sight he had made himself! What would the commanding officer say to such gallantry?" Martin laughed good-naturedly. He was so happy he could well afford to let them joke.

That night Martin was awaked from sleep. He saw before him Our Blessed Lord in glory, with the half of a military cloak in His hand, surrounded by adoring angels. The boy heard Him say: "Martin, yet a catechumen, has clothed Me with this garment!" The Saint's heart glowed within him. His love of Our Lord made him long to be baptized, that he might belong wholly to Him. When he was eighteen he received Holy Baptism, but remained some time in the army because of a great friend of his. After two years he left, and from that time to the day of his death, when he was very old, he grew in generosity towards God and man.

Think which kind of giving you like best, and then go and do likewise.

ST. GREGORY AND THE DEVILS

St. Gregory Thaumaturgus, November 17

I DON'T often think, speak, or write about devils, because I think the less we have to do with them the better. But now and then it is, perhaps, well to read what power they have, and how very much more power those have who are in God's grace and have Him on their side.

St. Gregory the Wonder-Worker was going out of his city, Cesarea. It was raining so hard that he had to stop and try to get shelter somewhere. There was no building near except a heathen temple, the most famous of all in the city. In it the devils had great honour paid to them, and they repaid their clients by answering questions, and pretending to foretell the future, which we all know the devil, clever as he is, cannot do. But he makes a very good guess sometimes which seems to do pretty nearly as well for many people. Before St. Gregory and his companions entered this temple the Saint made the sign of the Cross several times over the whole building. Then he went in and settled himself down for the night with his companions. Perhaps you think that means covering himself up, and finding as warm a spot as possible, and falling off to sleep as soon as he could. But it means nothing of the kind in this case. St. Gregory and those with him passed the whole night *praying*. You see I have written that in italics, as people find it such an out-of-the-way thing to do nowadays.

Next morning the little company set out on their journey, and at the appointed time the priests of the idols came back and began the ceremonies as usual. They sacrificed and prayed—but no answer came. On being urged, the devils acknowledged that they had been driven out by a man who had spent the night in the temple. The chief priest, in a fury, set off to find St. Gregory. When he had overtaken him he abused him violently for interfering with his worship, and threatened him with complaints to the magistrates unless he repaired the mischief he had done. St. Gregory was perfectly calm, and told the priest that he had power to drive away the devil, and power to bring him back. The pagan was amazed, and besought him to give him a proof of his power. St. Gregory took a slip of paper and wrote upon it: "Gregory to Satan: ENTER." These words were laid upon the altar of the idols, and, behold, Satan returned, and gave his false answers as before.

St. Gregory was a Saint, and God worked wonderful miracles by his hand. But I don't think any of his miracles is greater than what any one of you can work.

You can drive out the wicked spirit as truly as Gregory the Wonder-Worker did. Satan flies from the sign of the Cross made by your little hands, just as he fled from that made by the Saint. And, alas! like St. Gregory, you can say "ENTER!" and just as promptly he enters with his lying words. Is it not grand to have such a powerful weapon as the holy Cross? Because, you see, we may want to leave the devil alone. But he won't leave us alone, and we must have something to drive him away with. So when temptation comes, with its wiles and its soft colouring, and its coaxing manner, we will bravely make the sign of the Cross, and Satan will flee. May St. Gregory Thaumaturgus, the Wonder-Worker, teach you and me to put the devils to flight!

WHITBY'S QUEEN

St. Hilda, November 17

WHITBY's Queen was Hilda, grand-niece of St. Edwin, the King of Northumbria, whom St. Paulinus baptized. The holy prelate received Hereric, Hilda's father, and herself into the Church when the latter was fourteen years old. St. Aidan became her spiritual father, and directed her steps to Streaneshalch—that is, the "Bay of the Lighthouse," the name given at that time to Whitby. When I call Hilda "Queen of Whitby," you must not think I mean one who reigns like a Princess. Hilda became a nun, and founded a double monastery, where monks and nuns lived separate, but under one Superior, and that Superior generally was a woman. But Hilda was a true Queen, for she was obeyed by many subjects, directed an enormous establishment, and had fields and lands and cattle and fish. Wise people of all kinds came to visit her, and Kings often sought her counsel, for her wisdom was renowned far and near. Hilda loved peace, and it was her joy to reconcile differences and maintain charity. There is a beautiful story told of this wise Abbess and her herdsman, Cædmon. I will tell it to you.

One day there was a great feast in the Abbey of Whitby, and all the herdsmen were assembled in the open air, taking a grand repast that was provided for them by the hospitable nuns. The mead cup was passed round, and there were singing and music and dancing. Only one face was glum at the banquet; only one man passed the flowing cup on without tasting its contents; and when the meal was over, and in good earnest the songs began, the solemn-faced cowherd rose and quietly slipped away. Some few lusty young fellows shouted after him to know where he was going just as the fun of the evening was about to begin. But Cædmon did not answer. He hurried on his way with wet eyes. Then what was his grievance? He could not sing—only that. But that meant so much in those simple days. Every swain could compose and sing his rhymes with ease and joy, and anyone who refused was accounted churlish and poor company. But Cædmon could not sing; he was slow of wit, and he had no ear nor voice. He was sensitive, and where another herd would have laughed with the jesters, Cædmon blushed and fled. He fled to his cattle; they were his comfort; their soft dark eyes seemed to compassionate his sorrow, and their warm breath and rich red hides seemed to invite him to share the shelter. He lay down by the side of his favourite ox, pillowed his head upon the animal's sleek back, and fell asleep, soothed by the regular movement of the huge lungs.

Cædmon dreamed that he heard a voice; he listened. "Arise, Cædmon," it said, "and sing!" Cædmon, much surprised, said: "I cannot sing; for this I came away from the banquet and hid myself here in this shed far away from feast and laughter." "Sing, Cædmon!" the voice repeated; "sing to me!" Then it seemed to the herd that he raised himself upon his living pillow and sang—with such a rush of song that he was himself rapt with joy and intoxicated with the sound. Night passed away and the sun rose. Cattle move early, and Cædmon came to his senses. The wonderful dream came back to his mind, and he strode out upon the wide pasture-land to see if indeed he was endowed with angel song. And Cædmon rehearsed all he had sung in the glorious night-time; he sang of creation and the world of beautiful things about him. Slowly the news of the poet's gift was heard of about the land and reached the great Hilda's ears. One of her men, it was said, had been given an angel's voice to sing the wonderful works of God. She sent for the newborn poet, and he stood before her and her council in unabashed modesty. She questioned him about the voice he had heard in the night, and about the Divine command, and he told her faithfully and truly all that had passed in the cowshed the night before. Then Hilda bade him sing in God's Name once more. And Cædmon sang, and the music came and the words, and he neither faltered nor wearied. All the wise men of the council and Hilda herself were amazed at the wonderful song God had vouchsafed to the simple herdsman; and they praised God for His bounty and condescension. Then Cædmon was taught to write, that he might preserve to all time the story he had been taught in one night. And that story has come down to us, and we can all read what Cædmon sang that early morning before Hilda, the Queen of Whitby, and her wise men.

ST. ELIZABETH OF HUNGARY

November 19

S T. ELIZABETH was the daughter of a King and the wife of a powerful Prince. She was only twenty-four when she died, but in that short time she had suffered all kinds of misfortunes. When she was four years old she was sent away from her own home that she might be brought up in the Court of her future husband. The little child loved God better than anything in the world. So of course she loved prayer in the same way. She used to steal away from the amusements of the other children and find a quiet corner in the church. Others of the royal household did not like so much piety, and they used to make fun of Elizabeth and treat her cruelly. One day Elizabeth took off her diadem when she knelt before the Blessed Sacrament, and being asked why, she said she could not bear to wear jewels when she thought of the crown of thorns Our Lord had worn. But her young companion Agnes only sneered, and told her she was more fitted for the cloister than the throne.

Louis, the Landgrave, who was to be her husband,

Turned out.

did not think this, however. He loved Elizabeth and admired her for her great virtue, particularly for her love of the poor. She was allowed to spend anything she liked on them, and to attend them in the hospitals and in their homes. If this good young Prince had lived, Elizabeth would have suffered far less. But God took him Home and left Elizabeth a widow in her twentieth year. Then came all the troubles. The young Landgrave's relations turned the Saint out of doors, and left her without even the necessaries of life. She had no shelter for herself and her young children, until a pious woman took her out of the streets and gave her a night's lodging.

Though St. Elizabeth felt this trouble greatly, and her heart ached much, yet there was a secret joy within her. She knew that God sends sufferings to those He loves, and as she loved Him above all things, His love was what she wanted most in the world. So she suffered all without a word of complaint, and, what is very hard, without feeling any anger against those who had wronged her so shamefully. These Princes grew ashamed of their wicked behaviour, and restored Elizabeth to her castle and her honours and her wealth. The Saint was glad for many reasons. Now she could feed her poor again, and clothe them and shelter them. She built hospitals for them and dressed their wounds herself. Any day she might have been seen spinning wool for their garments and preparing food for their meals. Her father, the King of Hungary, wanted her to come back to his Court; he thought he could make her happier than she was in her late husband's castle. But for that very reason Elizabeth preferred to stay. She had learned to love contradictions and sorrow because they made her more like Our Lord Himself. Is not the love of God a great good? It changes the look of all things in life, and makes the hard easy, or at any rate easier to bear.

You all know the story of St. Elizabeth and the roses. One day the dear little Saint was coming down a steep path. Her mantle was filled and bulging out with food—meat, eggs, and fruit for the poor. Louis, her husband, coming home from the chase, met her and wondered to see her so laden. He blamed her for carrying such a load, and asked her to let him see what she had. She drew aside the mantle and laughingly replied: "Roses, my lord." The Landgrave looked in astonishment. Roses they were—fresh, blooming, beautiful roses. He took one out of the mass and kept it to the end of his life. Is not Our Lord lovingly kind? Try Him.

THE FEAST OF OUR LADY'S PRESENTATION

November 21

THE FEAST of the Presentation of Our Lady dates far back into the early ages. First it was kept by the Greeks—as the sermons of Greek patriarchs show. From them the festival spread into the West. A grand feast was celebrated at Avignon in 1372. And since the time of Sixtus VI, the office has been said by the Universal Church.

Tradition tells us that at the age of three, Anne and Joachim presented their little daughter in the Temple to serve the Lord till the time of her espousals. The Babe was left with the maidens, old and young, who had their home in the holy precincts. This presentation was no new custom special to Mary. Josaba, wife of Joiada, daughter of Joram, the King, hid little Joas the rightful King for six years *with her* in the Temple. And of Anna, the prophetess, St. Luke tells us "she was a widow until fourscore and four years, who departed not from the Temple night nor day, by prayers and fasting serving the Lord." She must have played with the

Babe Mary on her first coming into the Temple; and she must have taken her to her heart and helped to teach her how to serve God by prayer and fasting; for the maidens of the Temple had allotted tasks set them. There were priestly vestments to be made and mended, vessels to be polished, offices to be kept in order.

There has been published lately a lovely little dialogue, supposed to be spoken by old Anne and Joachim on their return to Nazareth from the Temple, where they had left their treasure. Anne, the holy Mother, is sad as sad can be. Joachim is of better heart.

Anne says:

> Talk not of home, my Joachim,
> For the light of our home is low and dim.
>
> Two are we that erst were three,
> Thou and I, and Babe Mary.
>
> O, the Lord's courts be great and fair,
> But who will play with my Baby there?
>
> Dost think the angels, Joachim,
> Will sing our sweet her cradle hymn?
>
> Or will the Lord of His gentle grace
> Lend one angel her mother's face?"

*   *   *   *   *

Joachim's answer is full of courage:

> Wife, thou wert glad but yester-eve,
> And wherefore now shouldst mourn and grieve?
>
> All of our three days' home-coming,
> The heart within thy breast did sing.

*   *   *   *   *

Dost repent that our hands have given
This, the crown of our life, to Heaven?

Hush thee, let not the good Lord know
Thou art grieved for serving Him so.

Did we not vow we would not hold
Back from His hand this finest gold ?

*   *   *   *   *

And Anne explains:

God's was she, and we gave her Him—
But—the house without her, Joachim!

Nay, I repent me not, my spouse,
But the heart is a-chill in the empty house.

And we are old, and it may be vain
To think we shall see our child again.

*   *   *   *   *

But Joachim holds to his point:

Anne, mother, weep not so:
What is God's to God doth go.

Wife, she danced in her lovely mirth
Joy more great than the joy of earth;

*   *   *   *   *

Danced on the altar steps in glee,
God's handmaid, our Babe Mary,

God's daughter beloved, and He
Holds in His arms our Babe Mary.

And in the end the sweet old couple say :

Be it done, O Lord,
To her according to Thy word!

The little piece is beautiful in its simplicity, and the
author, if he chances to see this quotation, must pardon

me the liberty I have taken. I would proudly give his name if I knew it!

There is an old custom on this feast to make fifteen genuflections towards the statue of Our Lady, reciting a Hail Mary at every step, in honour of the fifteen steps the Babe Mary took up the Temple stairs. The devotion is touching because it is commemorative, and wholesome because it is penitential!

DECEMBER

ST. FRANCIS XAVIER

December 3

St. Francis Xavier was a young nobleman who went to Paris to study and become great at the law; he was ambitious and wanted to make a name. But he learnt to know two friends, who showed him there was a better thing than a great name upon earth. Francis became a priest, a member of the Society of Jesus, and one of the greatest missioners who ever lived. Once he had a dream which returned time after time. He did not, of course, believe in dreams any more than we do, but this seemed like a prophecy of labours to come. He dreamt he was carrying an Indian on his shoulder up a very high mountain, over stony ground; the way was so steep and the burden so heavy that he groaned aloud and often woke the companion who slept with him. The dream came true: he carried many an Indian over steep ways up the Mount of God.

After his conversion, Francis's great desire was to be sent on the foreign missions. He would not ask the favour, for he wanted to do God's will and not his own.

But the two wills were one this time. Our Lord wished what the Saint was longing for. One day he received word from his great friend and master, Ignatius, that the Holy Father had chosen him to go to India to carry the Gospel to the natives there. This is what Ignatius wrote: "By higher counsels than those of our short-sighted judgment, Francis, you are destined to the mission of the Indies. The Sovereign Pontiff, to whom you have consecrated your obedience by vow, confers it on you; and I present it to you in his name. Accept it, however, as coming from the hand of God, who even from the East calls on *me* to send you thither, and on *you* to go."

Now, how much time do you think Xavier had to get ready? Just one day! Time enough to mend his old, worn-out habit, say good-bye to a few friends, and receive the Pope's blessing. When he came to say farewell to his dearest friend and father, Ignatius, the latter noticed how poorly he was clad. "What, Francis!" he said, "not a proper garment to cover you. Here, take this," and he took off an under waistcoat which protected his own chest from cold, and gave it to his dear son. Then Francis was ready indeed. He had his old habit on his back and his breviary under his arm. Remember, Francis Xavier was of noble birth, and had been brought up in luxury, for he was the youngest of a wealthy family, and his mother's darling. However, a little later Xavier had to accept another present, three coarse cloaks, one for himself and two for his two companions. The governor of the expedition wished to give the Saint an attendant to wait upon him on board ship, but Francis would not hear of such a thing. He was prepared to cook his own food, wash his own things, and clean anything he had in use. When people said that such work was beneath one of his rank, an Apostolic Nuncio, Xavier only smiled. He did not understand the arguments of the world.

I do not think either you or I can form any idea of the state of things on board ship in those days. The ships, or galleons, were of enormous size, divided into four or five storeys; sometimes there were eight hundred, sometimes a thousand on board. The voyage to India generally took six months. Provisions corrupted, water putrefied; such bad diet brought on fever, swellings, pestilence, sometimes madness. There were a thousand on board when Francis sailed, and they seemed to have been afflicted with more than the usual amount of illness. The patients lay on the deck, anywhere they could find a corner, with hardly a person to look after them. Then it was Francis's turn to show how full of love was his heart. "Thou shalt love thy neighbour as thyself," Our Lord said. But Francis went further than Our Lord's words: he followed His example and loved his fellow-men *better* than himself. He used to nurse the poor patients night and day; clean their sores, wash their poor linen, pray for them at their bedside, comfort and strengthen them to suffer bravely.

Goa was the Saint's first mission. He took a room in the hospital, so that he might be at the service of the sick. He portioned out his day between his labour thus: Three hours were given to sleep; this he took very often at the bedside of a patient, stretched on the floor. The rest of the night was given to prayer, and this refreshed him more, both in body and soul, than our sleep refreshes us; for the Saint was able to do much more than ever we can do with our natural rest. When morning dawned, Francis made his rounds, visiting each patient in the hospital and giving him relief in his sickness. Later in the day he said Mass, heard confessions, gave instructions, and preached in the churches or in the open air. On feast days he went round the town with a bell, and rang up the children to catechism. The little ones, two or three hundred in number, would follow him home and hear his instructions. With the children came the parents, and then there came a great change over the place. Men turned to God and began to understand that there is another world, and something beyond this worth living for.

Francis's one desire as he came to the end of his life was to go to China. He had overcome all sorts of difficulties—travel, expense, delay, threats; and just as he was within a few miles or so from the land of his desires Our Lord called him Home. He was stationed at Sancian, a little island where the Portuguese were allowed by the Chinese to land for purposes of commerce. The foreigners were forbidden to land in the *sacred* country of China itself, but the small island, or rather group of three islands, called Sancian, was the rendezvous for all traders to the Celestial Empire. Here Francis set to work to labour among the inhabitants, just as he laboured everywhere. There were merchants to convert, enemies to reconcile, pagans to bring to Baptism. A man named Vellio, a rich merchant, became great friends with Francis, and helped him with all his charities. One day the Saint was hard pressed. There was a poor orphan who had to be taken care of, but for whom no money was forthcoming. Xavier called on Vellio, but found he was out. He pursued him to the house of a friend, where Vellio was gambling. After a short discussion, the merchant gave his key to Francis and bade him go to his chest and take whatever sum he required—the more the better. Francis smiled and took the key. It opened a chest containing forty-five thousand ducats. Francis took three hundred scudi, quite a small sum, and carefully locked the chest. When Vellio found out what a paltry sum his friend had taken he was angry, and came to upbraid Francis. "I meant you to divide the sum between us, and you have taken a mere trifle," he said. Xavier looked into the man's earnest face and was touched to the heart. "Peter," he answered, "your offering is made in the sight of God, and He will measure it by your will. In His holy Name I promise you that never shall you come to want. You will be very near destitution, but at the last moment you will experience a change of fortune." The Saint's

words were fulfilled to the letter. Better still, from that
day Vellio, who had put his own pleasure before the
service of God, was a changed man.

There were no stately houses in Sancian; the Chinese
would not allow foreign merchants to build anything
substantial in the way of shelter on their territory. But
the Portuguese did their best for the habitation of the
Saint. They set him up a hut of wood and evergreens,
which was to serve him for a chapel, where Mass could
be said and confessions heard; and in and out went
Xavier all day long. He healed the sick and he raised
the dead to life. He foretold events buried in the future,
and he made the most wonderful conversions. But all
the time he was longing to sail for China—China,
where he was assured a certain martyrdom would await
him. But Our Lord had other designs for His dear
servant. He was to give up everything in this world,
even such a holy desire as to lay down his life for his
Faith. Xavier fell ill. His friends were good friends
indeed, but bad nurses. They applied remedies that
must have tried the Saint a hundred times more than
his fever. An unskilled hand bled him for a pain in his
side, and as a result his nerves contracted, causing him
untold suffering. He was taken from the ship, where
the rocking motion was too much for him, into a little
hut made of green boughs and carpeted with straw.
In his delirium he prayed, and his prayers were loving
ejaculations: " Jesus, Son of David, have mercy on me!"
"Show thyself a Mother!" "O Blessed Trinity!" It was

December 2, 1552, when he died. Looking at his crucifix, he cried out: "In Thee, O Lord, have I hoped; I shall not be confounded in eternity!" He was forty-six years of age, twelve of which he had lived as a Jesuit.

Make a picture of him. He was rather above the middle height; full and robust of body; pleasing and majestic of bearing; fair, with blue eyes. His hair was a chestnut colour, very thick, and he wore a beard. If any boy wants a patron who will help him to love God with all his heart, and serve Him all his days, let him choose this dear Saint, whose only love was God, and whose whole service was for his neighbour, for God's sake. So we will say, "Dear St. Francis Xavier, pray for us!

THE CRAB AND THE CRUCIFIX

More Stories of St. Francis Xavier

YOU would be inclined to think almost that a crab has as much to do with a crucifix as a walrus has with a carpenter. But mine is a true story, and the carpenter's is not—at least I, for one, never believed it. You have just read about St. Francis Xavier. This story comes in his life, which is full of wonders.

One day Francis, with seven of his companions, was cruising among the islands of Molucca. The burning sun was overhead, the calm, deep sea around. But as they sailed the pent-in waters near Baramara a terrible tempest arose. The boat in which St. Francis was tossed to and fro with every fresh wave, for it was a light vessel, ill-fitted to resist a squall. The native rowers, though accustomed to bad weather, gave themselves up for lost. But Francis calmly took from his neck the crucifix he always carried on his breast. He leant over the boat-side and dipped the cross in the seething water. Immediately there was a lull; the wind died down, the waters sank, the storm was over.

As Francis straightened himself up, the crucifix fell from his hand, slipped into the sea, and disappeared into the waves. The poor Saint was grieved beyond words. He could not be comforted; he had lost his greatest earthly treasure. But there was no use gazing into the water. The journey was continued. For twenty-four hours the Father and his little company sailed on, getting always farther and farther from the spot where the loss took place. At last they landed at the island of Talem, and he walked some hundred paces inland. Now I will use the language of one who saw the miracle with his own eyes, for he was one of the seven who were with Francis when he lost his crucifix.

"We both saw a crab issue from the sea carrying the identical crucifix upright, securely fixed in its claws; the creature made its way towards Francis, I being at the time close to his side. The Father knelt down and the crab remained quite quiet before him until he had taken away the cross, when it turned round and was soon lost sight of in the sea. After repeatedly kissing his re-found treasure, Francis remained as he was, with his arms crossed on his breast, in prayer for a full half-hour, I gladly joining with him in returning thanks to Our Lord Jesus Christ for this striking miracle. Then, rising up, we pursued our journey."

Do you see how Our Lord looks after His dear ones? Francis had left all for the love of Our Lord, and Our Lord looked after all things for Francis. We are not bound to believe in these miracles, you know—not absolutely bound; but to me it is the easiest thing in the world to believe, when a miracle like this one shows the courteous love of our dear Lord. I can see the same Master-hand in it that touched the little maiden and said, "Arise!" and, "Give her to eat!" Ah, children dear, we serve a good Master; only trust Him, and He will always stand by you in this world and the next.

FOR OR AGAINST?

The Seven Martyrs of Samosata, December 9

S AMOSATA was a splendid city on the River Euphrates.
The Euphrates is twin river to the Tigris, and
both flow through the land of the ancient Chaldees.
Maximian was Emperor over this part of the Eastern
world, and about the year AD 297 he returned victorious
from his campaign with the Persians. Flushed with
victory, he proclaimed a festival in honour of Fortune,
a Roman goddess. Her temple was to be rebuilt, he
said, and games instituted to do her honour. All the
people and magistrates of the city were to celebrate her
mysteries in the temple. When the day came there was
endless rejoicing; the whole city reeked with the smell
of burnt victims and the incense offered to the goddess,
who could neither see, nor hear, nor help.

In one of the finest mansions of the rich city, up in
a secret chamber, were two venerable men. They were
kneeling in prayer, their faces turned to the eastern
wall, upon which there was painted an image of the
Cross. Seven times a day they left their occupations
and prostrated themselves before the sign of their

redemption. This day they were not long together before five others joined them, young men and noble friends who loved the old magistrates as fathers. Shall I tell you their names? They are rather hard for our English tongue, and they sound very Eastern— Paragrus, James, Habibus, Romanus, and Lollianus. These Princes were not Christians, and they looked with amazement at the two, Hipparchus and Philotheus. What could they be doing with serious faces on such a glorious day as this? Why were they gloomily alone when all beside them were out in the glorious sunshine rejoicing?

Hipparchus answered that they were adoring their God, the Maker of Heaven and earth. One of the boys pointed with his finger at the lifeless picture on the wall, and asked them if that were their God. They listened attentively as the saintly old men explained the Faith; and when they had finished the five visitors asked to be made Christians. The old men explained that death, and a cruel death, was all they could look for in this world as followers of the Crucified; had they not better test their strength a while and defer their baptism? But the valiant five put their trust in God, and begged for the saving water.

That day a private messenger was sent to the priest James. The letter was sealed with the judicial seal, and it read as follows: "Be pleased to come as soon as possible, and bring with you a vessel of water and a Host and a horn of oil for anointing. Your presence is earnestly required by certain tender sheep which are come over to our fold and are impatient that our mark be set upon them." You see how cleverly the letter is worded. If it fell into the hands of spies they would not understand it, and the messenger would not get into trouble.

As soon as James received the letter he set out on foot to the beautiful mansion in the stately part of the city. He knew the seal well, and knew who had sent it. He covered the sacred vessels with his ragged cloak and hurried on his way. As he entered the house he said: "Peace be with you, servants of Jesus Christ, Who was crucified for His creatures." Then the five young men begged on their knees for baptism. They explained how they were ready to give up all for their Faith, that they knew how bitter would be their death, but that Our Lord and Saviour would help them in the struggle. After they had all prayed together for the space of an hour they made their submission to the Church, were baptized, and received Holy Communion. When the sacred rite was over, the priest took up the holy vessels again, hid them under his garment, and hurried through the streets home.

Meanwhile the festival was going on in the town; there were blowing of trumpets, slaughtering of victims, burning of incense, and riotous games. On the third day the Emperor happened to ask if all the magistrates had adored in the temple. Instantly an informer declared that the two chief officers, Hipparchus and Philotheus, had not taken part in the sacrifices for three years. Immediately an order was sent to the two friends to present themselves at the Temple of Fortune and offer incense to the idol. The seven confessors were together, but the messenger only sought the two judges. Hipparchus immediately received fifty stripes for answering the Emperor contemptuously about his gods. Philotheus was promised still higher offices in the court if he would offer incense, but he remained staunch and true. Both were manacled and sent to prison. After them came their five young friends. The Emperor tried persuasion and flattery; but the boys only smiled and stood firm. They were chained in separate dungeons, and kept without food till the festival was over.

You may imagine how those seven holy martyrs would pray for strength. They knew so well how dreadfully the Christians were persecuted, how slow was their torture, how malicious their executioners; and they would ask Our Lord to help them. What they most relied upon was the Holy Communion they had received. They told the Emperor that they could not dishonour their own bodies, because they had been nourished by the Body and Blood of Jesus Christ.

The Emperor had rich tents spread out upon the meadows that lay on the river's bank. Maximian's seat was high, and overlooked the spot where the sparkling Eiver Euphrates flowed to meet the Tigris. The trumpets blew, the crowd cheered as the Monarch in his imperial robes seated himself. Then came a sad procession: the two old magistrates were brought from prison with chains on their hands and feet; the other five followed with their hands tied behind their backs. They were asked the usual question, Would they sacrifice? and they answered "No." They were racked and scourged. Then they were sent back, all bleeding and torn; they were to see no one, and no comfort or relief was to be given to them. Their food was to be coarse bread, just enough to keep them alive. They lay in prison all by themselves, with no one to dress their wounds, with no one to say a kind word, for more than two months. Every day they expected to be taken before their judge, and to be either tortured again or put to death.

Just suppose these seven holy men had not learnt to pray or to make sacrifices, would they have been able to bear that trial, do you think? I am sure they would not. Some day, when they felt very weak and discouraged, they would have stopped the jailer and told him that they had reconsidered the matter, and were ready to do the imperial will. Then they would have been taken out of prison with all honour; the Emperor would have said some gracious words to them, and they would have been restored to their property. But then! They would have bought time by the loss of eternity, and that is a mighty poor bargain, and not worth considering for one moment.

And the two valiant confessors did not hesitate one moment. When the beautiful June sun was making the waters of the Euphrates gleam like gold, the seven men were brought before the Emperor. They were reduced to skeletons; they could scarcely walk; they were more like dead than living men. Maximian looked compassionately at them. He told them that if they would give in he would have them taken to a warm bath, their hair should be shorn, and their wounds healed. They begged he would not try to rob them of their crown. Then his anger broke into a fury. "Wretches!" he screamed. "You seek death and you shall find it!" He commanded cords to be tied round their mouths and bound round them, so that they should not be able to speak. A procession was formed, and they were conducted to the place of execution. Then was shown how much these good masters were loved. Their friends and servants came, and made a sort of escort, bewailing them and openly showing their displeasure at their execution. Some of the most powerful of the citizens got leave to make one more attempt to win them over. They untied their cords, took them into a sheltered spot, and implored of them to pretend to adore. But the seven holy men raised up their voices to praise God and bless Him for all His benefits.

At the place of execution the Emperor was present to see them die. Seven crosses were set up over against the gate of the city. The martyrs were hoisted up and left to their fate. Some Christian ladies came, and, by bribery, were allowed to wipe their agonized faces. Hipparchus expired after a short struggle; two died the next day, and the rest were taken down alive and cruelly tortured.

Now, children, such a story makes our blood run cold. We shrink from pain, from discomfort even. How should we endure such-like suffering? All we can say is that we have not to bear it yet. And if Our Lord sent us the pain, He would send us the grace to bear it. In the meantime we have to bear our little troubles and little griefs with great patience and for the love of God. Nothing helps so much to do big things as doing little ones as well as ever we can; not only pretty well, but *as well as ever we can*. We'll remember that, won't we?

ADVENT

CHRISTMAS has not yet come, but it is very near—so near that we can smell the plum-puddings, the mince-pies. We hear of special shopping; we ourselves are busy planning presents and anticipating them. Shopkeepers have long since made their shops look smart and festive. They are busy behind the counters or at the till. School-children are on the verge of going home; their holidays soon begin. So we are all a little excited, and more than a little eager. Now, if I were to ask you what would you like best in all the world for a Christmas present, what would you answer? Of course it would be a silly question for me to ask, for I have not a sixpence in the world to buy a present for one of you, much less for all of you. Still, I cannot help wondering what you would like.

I know what a mouse would say if it were asked. "A big cheese, please, and to be left in peace to enjoy it—no cat near nor meddling cook." Jack Horner would say: "A Christmas pie and a quiet corner to eat it in." And he would add: "Don't bother about a spoon or fork; I can use my thumb." Little Bo-Peep would like her sheep safe and sound with all their tails behind them; Jack Sprat would like lean meat, and his wife would like the fat; and so the nursery-rhyme people would go on.

But, then, what would you like? That question is not yet answered. Well, since I cannot get it answered by you, I will tell you what I would like for you. I would like the Holy Child to give you two gifts, and if you get anything better than those, please let me know as soon as possible. The two gifts are the *spirit of prayer* and *generosity*. Now, don't be frightened. I don't mean that I want you to do nothing but pray, for you would pray very badly if you did *nothing* but that. Only that you should love prayer, spend the proper time in it well; make it as much a business as a study, or work, or eating, or sleeping. A little girl of about eight was asked what was man. She answered: "An animal that prays." I think that was a very beautiful answer. Let us be men according to that definition.

The other gift I want for you is *generosity*, a love of giving—not of spending, mind. Some children think they are very generous because they can make money fly. That is no proof at all. That is the proof of a spendthrift, not of a generous person. To give to the poor, to the old, to the delicate, to the weak, to the younger ones, to those who cannot give in return, to unattractive people, to our enemies—this is generosity. And you see it need not mean money—that is the best of it. Some of us have not a coin of the realm in our possession, but still we give. There is a child I know who saves up and hands over to one she loves her precious savings for the poor. She could give it herself, but she wants to give up even the pleasure of spending. That child will have a sweet reward in heaven! Some poor little things were brought to have warm stockings put on their tiny legs at Christmas time. They were very ragged, very dirty, very forsaken little babes. But would you believe it! most of them had a halfpenny in their wee hands for "the Infant Jesus"! On Christmas Day I shall spend a particular time at the crib asking our dear little Saviour to give you children those two beautiful gifts—the love of prayer and generosity.

deep silence all around; you could only hear the soft breathing of the cattle and the slight rustle of the straw as of someone moving gently. Then my eyes closed for a moment, and when they opened again there was a brilliant light in the poor stable, a radiant, shining light, and its bright rays came from where the manger stood against the rough wall. And as I looked I saw through the brightness a lovely Babe sleeping. Its tiny hands were crossed upon Its breast; Its little feet rested upon the spiky straw; Its fair hair curled over Its white, white forehead; Its eyelashes drooped upon Its cheek. By Its side there knelt Its Mother; her hands were clasped, her head bowed in adoration. A little way off there stood a strong man whose eyes wandered from the beautiful Mother to the tiny Babe. He was alert to wait upon either of them, to guard and guide them both. I knew where I was; I knew the time of night; I knew the Mother and the Child; I knew the guardian standing near. My tongue did not speak, nor my lips move, but my heart was aglow and it seemed to join in the Divine silence of the night.

But my head drooped for an instant; it was only a human head. When I lifted it again I saw through the open door a band of white-robed children coming into the grey stable. They were tiny creatures, some of them; and none of them were big. But oh, what joy! Their little faces beamed! In their hands they waved golden palms, and they sang a glorious hosanna in soft childish treble. In they trooped, in twos and threes, or one by one as the fancy took them; but they had but one thought between them—to make for the manger. So on they glided, bowing to the Virgin Mother as they passed, and touching with loving veneration the strong man's hand. Around the manger the white band hovered, getting closer, drawing nearer to the sleeping Babe, and as they took their places in rows about Him, the Child awoke. Oh! then there burst from Him such a smile of welcome, such a look of love, as He drew each baby to Him and kissed its soft cheek with His own red lips! In the distance stood shadowy mothers, whose eyelids were scarcely dry, but upon whose faces there shone the light from the manger. Who were these glorious little ones? Will the big ones tell our little ones? They can guess my dream's meaning better than I, perhaps.

Complete in 5 Volumes

Stories of the Saints for Children
by M. F. S.
Originally published between 1874 and 1878

The stories of over 180 saints, told for children.

Volume One: Well-Known and Beloved Saints
St. Francis & Clare—St. Anthony—St. Benedict—St. Dominic
St. Ignatius—St. Cecilia—St. Agnes—St. Teresa

Volume Two: More Beloved Saints
St. George—St. Patrick—St. Simon Stock—St. Louis
St. Agatha—St. Lucy—St. Dorothy—St. Bernard

Volume 3: Bishops, Apostles and Evangelists
St. Martin—St. Augustine—St. Boniface—St. Peter—St. Paul
St. Andrew—St. Stephen—St. Mary Magdalene

Volume 4: Fathers & Doctors of the Church
St. Ambrose—St. Hilary—St. Jerome—St. Leo the Great
St. Gregory the Great—Venerable Bede

Volume 5: Saints of the Age of Faith
St. Anselm—St. Hildegard—St. Peter Damian—St. Odilo
St. Norbert—St. Bonaventure—St. Thomas Aquinas

Plus 3 bonus volumes:

Stories of Martyr Priests
Edmund Campion—Robert Southwell—Henry Walpole

Stories of Holy Lives
St. Margaret Mary—Blessed Imelda—St. John Berchmans
Ven. Anna Maria Taigi—Anne Catherine Emmerich—St. John Vianney

Legends of the Saints (Short tales for Young Children)
Robin Red-Breast—Our Lady of Guadalupe—The Christmas Rose
The Legend of St. Christopher—St. Francis and the Wolf

www.ingramcontent.com/pod-product-compliance
Lightning Source LLC
Chambersburg PA
CBHW031830090426
42741CB00005B/189